D1006690

Praise for Women's Worth

"Eleanor combines two areas that can change the fiscal well-being of America and America's families: women becoming financially competent, and creating women's circle gatherings as a way to talk, learn, and share about money. *Women's Worth* stands out because of Eleanor's passion about women's financial well-being, her empathy, and her professional mastery of financial planning. The journey to financial maturity is a worthy path and this book will serve as a compassionate guide, inspiration, and map."

— Elizabeth Jetton, CFP®
Partner, RTD Financial Advisors
Past President, The Financial Planning Association

"In her very readable and engaging book, Eleanor Blayney connects all the dots between how women are unique from men in our orientation to money, and how we need to reorient ourselves to assure our financial futures and our ability to exercise our full power as women."

— Dianne Chasen Lipsey
President, Sewall Belmont House and Museum

"While there have been many books written to help women with their investing and financial needs, not one of them, in my opinion, comes close to cutting through the BS and saying it like it *really* is for us girls. I've been in the investment advisory business for 20 years and always knew there was a better way to work with women, but didn't have the time or clear thinking until now to focus on how to articulate it. Eleanor articulates this 'better way' as well as anyone could, and I'm so glad it's been done. I am quite sure women investors and advisors will get a ton out of this book."

— Margie Carpenter, CFP®, CIMA®
Principal, Bell Tower Advisors

"With *Women's Worth*, Eleanor gives readers an extraordinarily helpful guide. She combines the soft and hard sides of making important financial decisions into a practical reference that should have a long and useful life."

— Mark Tibergien
CEO, Pershing Advisor Solutions

"Eleanor Blayney is a wonderful thinker and a great writer. With *Women's Worth*, she shows she understands the new financial realities for women."

— Deborah Nixon, Ph.D.
Founder, Trust Learning Solutions

WOMEN'S WORTH

WOMEN'S WORTH

Finding Your Financial Confidence

ELEANOR BLAYNEY, CFP®

Direction$, LLC,
McLean, VA

ISBN 978-09843618-2-3

Publisher's Cataloging-in-Publication Data

Blayney, Eleanor.
Women's worth : finding your financial confidence / Eleanor Blayney.
p. cm.
ISBN 978-09843618-2-3
Includes bibliographical references and index.
1. Women—Finance, Personal. 2. Finance, Personal. 3. Investments. 4. Financial security.
I. Title.

HG179 .B54 2010
332/.024—dc22 2009913073

First Edition

Direction$, LLC
7230 Aynsley Lane
McLean, VA 22092

Copies of this book may be purchased for educational, business, or promotional use. Please contact Eleanor@directionsforwomen.com.

Printed in the U.S.A.

For all my Elizabeths (daughter, sister, and mother),
and for my sister Sarah

"I think I am supposed to know this stuff . . ."
—from conversations with women everywhere,
talking about personal finance

CONTENTS

Preface

When I was born, almost everyone in my family hoped for and expected a boy. I was the last child after a trio of girls, and for nine months friends and family had their bets on a boy. Alas, my birth made it four of a kind.

Nevertheless, my father was joyful upon my arrival. Family legend has it that when our housekeeper offered him her condolences upon his return from the hospital, he fired her. He loved his girls.

My father made us proud of our female identity. He used to love to tell stories about his many pranks and adventures as a boy, but would always start the same way: "When I was a little girl . . ." I would giggle and scold him: "Oh Daddy, you were never a girl!" But listening to his stories, I decided that being a girl must be so special that even a grown man wished he were one.

My father taught me that, as a girl, I could be strong and independent. After I finished high school he wanted me to apply to Yale the first year that that university began accepting women undergraduates. I was flattered by his confidence, but attended Mount Holyoke College instead, one of this country's first all-women's institutions of higher learning. I went on to complete graduate school at one of the first all-women's colleges in the United Kingdom—Girton College, University of Cambridge. At these schools I never had to worry about being too smart or asking dumb questions. As a result, I became convinced of the power of learning with and from women.

About twenty years later I found myself the sole female partner in a four-principal financial planning firm. We worked hard and built a successful practice that managed over a billion dollars in assets for hundreds of clients. Our business grew primarily by referrals, and I began to see a pattern in the prospects calling and asking for me. For the most part, they were women, referred by other women. What I had experienced in college and graduate school was repeating itself in my business: when trying to master technically complex subjects, such as finance and handling money, women learn best when talking to other women.

It is this unique female perspective and approach that I try to capture in *Women's Worth: Finding Your Financial Confidence.*

I bring to this task not only my knowledge as a financial planner, but the real-life stories of my clients and my experience with my own financial ups and downs: my marriage and divorce; funding my daughter through college and grad school (but that was it!); building a business, selling a business, starting a new one; retiring from one career and launching another; taking care of elderly, ailing parents and settling their estates. I have drawn on just about everything I know as a financial planner and a woman and have tried to ensure that the former honors and serves the latter.

Please join me in this woman-to-woman talk about finance.

Introduction

Women Ask for Directions

An "Aha!" moment came to me as I stood before an auditorium full of alumnae from Mount Holyoke College, an all-women's liberal arts school nestled in the low hills of central Massachusetts. They had gathered on campus one fall weekend to learn about fundraising, and I had been asked to address the topic of philanthropy.

My talk was titled "How Much Is Enough?" It was one I had given many times before. I discussed the themes of capacity and confidence. *Capacity* is having the ability to give as a result of wealth accumulation through proper financial planning. *Confidence* is having the know-how to be smart about giving: knowing how to make gifts other than cash, for example, or how to perform due diligence on recipient organizations or receive a return on an investment in non-profit activities. Because my audience was made up of women only, I also threw in some statistics and anecdotes about women's patterns of giving which, perhaps not surprisingly, are different from men's.

After wrapping up, I felt my speech had been a success. The audience had been nodding in agreement throughout, and when it was time for questions, hands went up immediately.

The questions surprised me. I had been expecting this well-educated group to raise some difficult issues—about the new legislation on making gifts directly from an individual retirement account (IRA) to a charity, or the use of remainder trusts. Instead, they seemed stuck on the first half of my speech, the part about the need for financial planning. And their questions were fundamental: "Who can I talk to about my 401(k), insurance, or my business?" "How do I get my mother to tell me about her finances?" "How do I find a good planner?" These women were obviously hungry for financial information and advice, and eager to find an advisor they could trust.

My "Aha!" moment was, therefore, more of an "Oh dear!" moment. I had, of course, been aware that the financial planning profession had traditionally ignored women, along with minorities and economically disadvantaged populations. The profession primarily focuses on the wealthy, which has historically meant white males. But I had believed that, with an increasing number of women in the workforce, this was changing.

Since the 1970s, more women have been participating in the labor force than ever before. There are now more female executives, billionaires, and leaders. We recently came pretty close to having a female president. Women now control more than half of the country's private wealth.

As the enormous transition of wealth from the Second World War generation to the baby boomers continues, women—who statistically live longer than men—will ultimately inherit this wealth too. As a result of all this social and economic change, I had assumed that women, out of necessity and self-regard, were beginning to think more about financial matters. I had thought that the traditional roles of "Dad does the investing and Mom does the shopping" had been left behind.

Apparently not. Or not as quickly as I would have hoped.

Among the group I addressed at Mount Holyoke College were some of the best-educated women in the country. They were scientists, business owners, association managers, and elected officials. They were wealthy. They were involved in their communities and were not afraid to ask questions. But while they had capacity, in the way I defined this term above, they lacked the confidence to be financial decision-makers.

To say that I first became aware of this female crisis of financial confidence that day at Mount Holyoke would be a stretch. I had sisters and female friends who cheerfully admitted they were "hopeless at that stuff." One acquaintance who belonged to every type of women's group going—book group, cooking group, Pilates class—had told me there was only one remaining taboo when it came to women's conversations, and that was money. She and her friends talked freely about sex, health, and relationship issues, but no one was prepared to talk about net worth, credit card debt, or balancing a checkbook. Surely it was not shame that kept them silent—not in today's reality show culture, where it seems the more open the better. I concluded that it had to be fear—fear of not knowing, and being seen to not know.

But until that day I had discounted the depth and breadth of that feminine fear. In my financial planning practice I have become used to working with women who have taken the bold step of seeking professional advice. Fear may have propelled them to my office, but they had chosen not to stay stuck in their money anxieties. What I didn't realize was that the women I serve are not typical. My clients, it turns out, are the minority. Outside my advisory orbit the real crisis of confidence was taking place.

A 2006 study conducted by Allianz Life Insurance on women, money, and power provides the statistical proof of this lack of confidence. Ninety percent of the 1,925 women respondents ages twenty-one to over sixty reported feeling insecure when it came to personal finance. These were not women who suffered inferiority complexes in other aspects of their lives. Sixty-five percent assessed themselves as sensitive, 51 percent as perceptive, and 46 percent as intuitive. However, when asked about these same characteristics—sensitivity, perceptiveness, and intuition—regarding money and investing, the percentages plummeted. Only 7 percent reported themselves to be sensitive, 13 percent perceptive, and 11 percent intuitive about money issues.

Because women as a demographic are becoming wealthier, the major financial service firms—brokerages, insurance companies, and banks—are beginning to target women as a promising market. But while they pay a lot of lip service to the idea that women are a distinct market, the advice offered and the way it is offered are seldom specific to women. In reality, women face financial risks distinct from those faced by men. Their attitudes toward risk are also different. More importantly, women's styles of communication and ways of learning are different. Women feel more comfortable and more empowered when talking to other women about money and its meaning and role in their lives. A financial world long dominated by men uses a language of gain and loss, winning and losing that does not translate well into women's experiences and understanding of wealth. Therefore, financial planning advice and the way that advice is delivered has to be different for women than for men.

CAN YOU RELATE?

"I always say that personal finance has been taught by old white men for old white men for way too long."—I Will Teach You to Be Rich, Ramit Sethi

I wrote *Women's Worth* hoping to get women from all walks of life talking about and feeling comfortable with their money. I want to provide a uniquely female perspective to ignite conversation and create a sense of financial community that might bridge the gap between women's financial capacity and their confidence, between what they have now and what they can hope to have in the future if they are shown how.

Since I began this project, the financial world has changed profoundly. We have experienced an unprecedented meltdown of wealth and erosion of trust. At times I feared that my subject, too, was evaporating. Who wants to talk about money that we feel we no longer have? On the other hand, a changing economic order may allow for a new conversation about finance, one that may be more accessible to women, one that speaks to them in and on their own terms. It has even been suggested that the old masculine rules of financial management have failed us and that women's ways of thinking about risk, return, and financial security may provide a new paradigm for financial advice in this new millennium.

CAN YOU RELATE?

Georgetown University professor and sociolinguist Deborah Tannen, in the audio series He Said, She Said, *tells the story of a female medical student who received a poor performance review from her supervisor. "Why?" asked the student of her supervisor. He told her that it was because she didn't know as much as the others, who were all male. When she asked why he drew this conclusion, he said, "Because you ask so many questions."*

Chapter One

Women Discuss—How and Why Our Conversation about Personal Finance Needs to Be Different

So much of financial planning involves assessments about risk. The financial risks that women run, and their ways of dealing with those risks, are distinct from men's. This is due to very real biological, psychological, and cultural distinctions, including the following:

- Women live longer.
- Women are likely to suffer financial setbacks as a result of divorce, whereas men are more apt to be financially better off.
- Women are far more likely to live by themselves for a significant period of time, either by choice or circumstance.
- Women's workplace participation is more intermittent than men's, resulting in greater gaps in insurance and benefit coverage and reduced opportunity to save for retirement.
- Though better educated than we once were, women still gravitate toward traditionally female career choices—teaching or administrative work—because these jobs afford more possibility of part-time hours or accommodation for family demands.

- Women do most of the caretaking of dependents, both children and the elderly.
- Women are more risk-averse than men when it comes to investing.
- Women are generous by nature, but more timid about making significant gifts.

To take an example, imagine an average sixty-five-year-old male retiree who has managed to put away $1 million in assets to retire on for the rest of his life. His portfolio is invested 60 percent in stocks. Using a method of analysis called Monte Carlo simulation (as incorporated into a program from T. Rowe Price Associates, Inc.), we can estimate there is an 80 percent probability that he will not run out of money if he keeps his monthly expenses to $4,300. If he lives a bit higher off the hog—at $5,000 a month—the likelihood that he will not run out of money before he runs out of life drops to 60 percent.

Why the conversation needs to be different for women

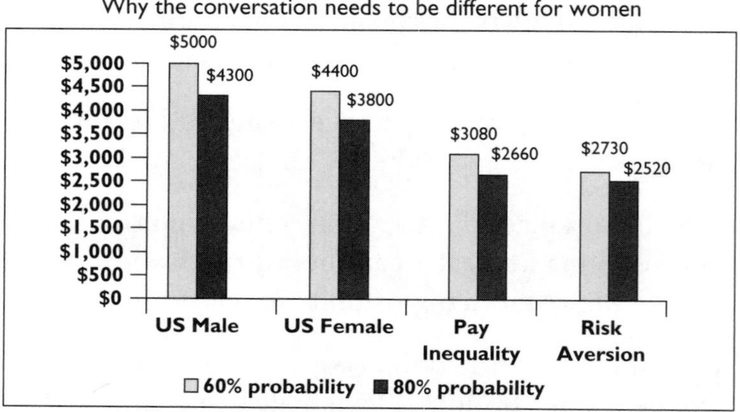

Graph shows expected monthly income, at two probability levels, based on initial retirement period of 25 years for a male, a $1,000,000 portfolio, invested 60% in stocks. Female assumed to live 5 years longer, save 70% of what male saves, and invest 25% in stocks.

If our retiree is a woman, however, the results look quite different. Because she is likely to live at least five years longer than her male counterpart, the amount of money she can live on with a 60 percent likelihood of not running out is only $4,400 a month. For an 80 percent probability, she has to cut back to $3,800 a month—which effectively results in a 12 percent gender tax.

Now suppose she has not been able to save as much as our male retiree, perhaps because she was paid less for the same work, or because her workforce participation was interrupted to raise children or take care of elderly parents. As a result, she has managed to save only 70 percent of what the man has saved. Simple math results in a new income of $3,080 a month with a 60 percent probability of not running out of money, or $2,660 a month with an 80 percent probability.

Now suppose further that rather than holding 60 percent of her retirement portfolio in stocks, our female retiree invests only 25 percent in stocks. Studies have shown that women invest less aggressively than men. Her monthly income now decreases to $2,730 with a 60 percent probability of not running out, or a mere $2,520 if she wants to have an 80 percent probability. We already know from her investment choices that she wants to play it safe, so she would likely settle for the lesser monthly amount. Few sixty-five-year-old women, however, would feel comfortable with $2,520 per month to live on.

Clearly, financial planning for women requires different assumptions and different analyses. The tools we use to get them to their goals need to be less blunt and more adaptable to their particular circumstances. Traditional financial planning does not pay enough attention to these uniquely female circumstances.

Research has shown that men prefer to learn independently, while women learn well in supportive, collaborative environments.

How we talk about finances to women also needs to change. Women perceive and learn differently from men. In particular, research has shown that men prefer to learn independently, while women learn well in supportive, collaborative environments. Men are apt to charge ahead and learn while doing, whereas women prefer to stand back, listen, and observe. They want to read the manual, so to speak, before turning on the computer or launching the program.

The field of sociolinguistics, and more particularly, the work of Deborah Tannen, professor of linguistics at Georgetown University, shows that men are much more comfortable speaking in terms of "one-up" or "one-down." They have an inherent need for competition and hierarchy in order to understand where they fit in the world. Women, on the other hand, are much more collaborative: they seek common experience and want to put themselves on the same emotional and intellectual plane as others.

The male need for hierarchy, for locating themselves in the pecking order, may explain why the language of personal finance—and most particularly that of investing, long dominated by men—is invariably put in terms of winning and losing. It may explain, too, why my male clients are more apt to evaluate investment performance in terms of benchmarks. They want to know if they have done better or worse than a given standard, such as the S&P 500 or the Dow, whereas female clients, when presented with investment results, are more apt to ask: "But what does this mean?" And they are not asking for that meaning to be measured in basis points.

Women are more contextual and less absolute than men. In my experience, they want the context for advice and find it easier when I preface my counsel, as I invariably do, with the phrase: "It depends." It depends on your risk tolerance; it depends on your family situation; it depends on where you want to live. My male clients are less patient with context and usually want more definitive, shorter answers. They want the bottom line. Men are the ones who, when asked by their wives or girlfriends if they look good in a certain dress, will simply answer "Sure" or "Nope." Women know, of course, that the better answer begins with another question, such as: "What do you have to go with it?" or "Where do you plan to wear it?"

How can women's preferences for commonality, context, and consensus be brought to bear on financial advice? The answer, I strongly believe, lies in "circles", the process of women coming together with a common purpose. Throughout history, women have been attracted by the productive potential of circles. In colonial times, women gathered for sewing circles or quilting bees to assist in setting up the household of a couple about to be married or to have a child. Yesterday's sewing circles and bees have evolved into today's book clubs, recipe swaps, scrapbooking clubs, giving circles, and investment groups. The popularity of these groups among women is unquestioned and growing.

A circle setting where women come together to discuss the financial issues unique to them, such as living alone or coping with the negative financial consequences of divorce, is immensely empowering.

Learning about money in a community of women makes the work seem easier and even enjoyable. A circle setting where women come together to discuss the financial issues unique to them, such as living alone or coping with the negative financial consequences of divorce, is immensely empowering. It is also a safe place to discover one's financial identity and to find answers to what women may fear are dumb questions. Through sharing and relating, women gain autonomy and knowledge to bridge the gap between their capacity and confidence.

I am so convinced of the power of financial planning circles that, in 2008, I started a business that offers personal finance workshops around the country to groups of women ages forty to sixty-five. These women have financial means, but, due to various historical and cultural factors, they need help in using their money to achieve their desired financial ends. My intent for these circles is to teach women to become financially savvy through a curriculum that reflects women's unique learning styles and their appetite for relationship and shared experience. The company is called Directions, LLC. We all know that women, unlike most men, are willing to ask for directions. As Merrill Lynch executive Robert Doll observed: "Women know what they don't know and aren't afraid to ask for help." Women also are willing to take directions with a readiness that is not characteristic of men.

Not all women have the time or inclination, however, to attend a circle on a regular basis. It is for them that I have written *Women's Worth*. This book is an attempt to initiate a dialogue and provide some of the answers to questions that constitute the subject matter of circles, to be accessed whenever and wherever women readers have time.

Competent financial planners can also play critical supporting roles. Circles empower women to seek better answers to their unique issues, but many answers can also be found by consulting a trusted advisor. Should that advisor be a woman? I have been a CERTIFIED FINANCIAL PLANNER™ professional for more than two decades and can say unequivocally that some of the best planners I know are women. Many have the extraordinary ability to think from the middle of their brains—drawing on the linear, logical left-brain thinking that is so necessary for financial analysis and strategy, as well as right-brain creativity that keeps them vital and innovative in the eyes of their clients. One woman CFP® professional, who was a private detective before becoming a planner, put the secret to her success much more simply: "In both cases, being able to listen very carefully is essential."

Currently only one in four CFP® professionals is a woman. While women are increasingly asking for women advisors, the supply of competent female professionals is simply not large enough to meet the potential demand, so what must change is the way the profession as a whole reaches out to women. Planners need to address the issues of most concern to women, using language and concepts that really speak to them.

Decision Point ***How do I choose a financial planner?***

Just thirty years ago, few people knew what financial planning was all about, and fewer still had ever talked to a financial planner. Today, financial planning has all the hallmarks of an established and respected profession. There are many financial planning designations, but the gold standard among them is the CERTIFIED FINANCIAL PLANNER™ mark or the CFP® designation, which signifies that the holder has passed a rigorous exam and met initial and ongoing requirements in the areas of education, experience, and ethics. A planner who fails to meet these requirements or violates certain standards can temporarily or permanently lose the right to use the CFP® designation. Practitioners are overseen, and professional standards enforced, by the Certified Financial Planner Board of Standards, a regulatory and licensing association based in Washington, DC. There are also membership associations for financial planners, such as the Financial Planning Association (FPA) and the National Association of Personal Financial Advisors (NAPFA), which seek to educate the public about financial planning.

Any of these organizations can provide guidance in finding a competent financial planner in good standing. The CFP® Board's search engine at www.cfp.net allows you to enter the name or location of a CFP® to determine the individual's certification status, whether they are currently practicing, and if they have been publicly disciplined by the Board. The websites of the FPA (www.fpanet.org) and the NAPFA (www.napfa.org) provide information on their members' specialties within the profession, such as debt management, comprehensive financial planning, or divorce planning. All three organizations also provide generic guidance on the appropriate questions to ask when interviewing planners.

Should you seek a female CFP® professional? There is a practical answer to this question, as well as a subjective one. As mentioned, male CFP® practitioners still outnumber female CFP® practitioners, so from a pure numbers point of view, it will be easier to find a good male advisor. From the subjective vantage, do you prefer to go to a gynecologist who is a woman?

Would you go to an unmarried priest for marriage counseling? Is it important to you that your advisors really understand what you are talking about because they themselves have experienced it?

For some of us, empathy is not gendered, and that's fine. A sense of shared female experience is less important than competence and expertise. Others, however, want to talk to someone who knows what it's like to give birth, or, in this case, to face gender differences in the financial and business world. They don't just want a competent, experienced individual who makes financial decisions; they want a competent, experienced *woman* to make those decisions.

The National Program on Women and Aging advises taking the following key steps when seeking a planner:

1. Interview more than one financial planner.

2. Prepare questions and a statement of assets and liabilities (see page 37) before the interviews.

3. Ask to see a copy of a financial plan previously prepared by the planner.

4. Investigate the planner by checking credentials and their status with regulatory organizations.

5. Be clear from the outset how the planner will be paid and what their services will cost you.

A survey conducted by the National Program found that very few women undertook any of the above steps when choosing a planner. These women were definitely concerned with finding a professional they could trust, but few had any ideas about how to go about it. Half simply took the recommendation of a relative or friend. Only 9 percent did background checks to see if the planner had any professional sanctions (i.e., disciplinary actions.) The planner's experience, qualifications, or record of service were virtually ignored. Furthermore, nearly half the survey respondents (43 percent) admitted that they had not discussed compensation before work began.

In this area more than any other, you cannot be afraid of asking too many questions. At a minimum, this is the information you should obtain from a prospective planner:

- A copy of the planner's Form ADV (the annual filing the planner files with the U.S. Securities and Exchange Commission (SEC) or the state securities authority if she or he provides investment advice). Read it. It's dull, but it will describe in detail the planner's services, clientele, and compensation.

- Any pending or settled litigation or arbitration cases that the planner is involved in. Ask what organizations the planner is regulated by and contact these organizations for a background check. If your advisor is a registered representative with a broker-dealer, the Financial Industry Regulatory Authority (FINRA) is the organization to contact. If the planner offers investment advice, he or she should be registered with the SEC or a state securities commission. If the planner is a CFP® professional, the CFP® Board of Standards will have a record of any public sanctions the board has taken against the planner.

- Their years of experience and employment history (this information is also included in the Form ADV).

In addition, here are some suggested questions to help you evaluate whether the planner will be a good fit for you:

- Does she have personal experience with any of the financial events you are concerned about? If you are worrying about the financial impacts of a divorce, for instance, ask if she herself is divorced. (You might also ask if she is willing to share whether her divorce was a "good" or a messy one.) If you are interested in starting a business, ask what her experience as an entrepreneur or business owner has been.

- Does he use income-based or asset-based financial planning software? What you want to know is whether the planner is primarily concerned with asset management or whether he is also able to assist you with income and expense management. If you have a spending problem or need help with budgeting and taxes, a planner who specializes only in investments and portfolio management may not be the best advisor for you.

- What will your relationship entail in year one? How many meetings? Who will be at the meetings? Who will be your contact person? How frequently will you be contacted? When it comes to relationships, women need to know who will be calling whom and when.

- What will your relationship entail in later years? How many meetings? Is it likely that you will still be working with the same planner? What is the career path for professionals in the planner's firm?

- How, if at all, does she change assumptions or strategies when planning for a woman rather than a man?

- Are his female clients primarily widows? One of a couple? Single professionals? Business owners?

- If your values focus on family or legacy: How much intergenerational planning does she do, and of what type? How often does she work with parents and/or children of her clients?

- If your values include community and charitable planning: How does he participate in the non-profit community? Does he serve on any not-for-profit boards? What kinds of charitable gifts has he helped his clients make?

- If your values include self-development or maximizing your earning potential: Does she have life-coaching skills or has she used, or referred clients to, professional coaches? Ask, too, whether she has helped with contract or salary negotiations or if she has expertise in business and employee benefits.

- What types of financial issues or situations does he refer to other professionals? For example, an attorney must prepare estate-planning documents, even if your planner helps you think through how you would like your estate handled and distributed. If the issues he refers out are issues you will need help with, ask if he could give you the name of a client who has used these references. Call this client and ask how the referral was handled. Was the client satisfied? Did the planner stay in the loop with the other professional?

- What efforts does she make to educate her clientele? Does she offer seminars? Does she recommend any books or periodicals? Does she provide e-mail bulletins?

- What concrete examples can he provide of ways his advice has benefited his clientele?

- How many clients does she handle? Ask if you are typical. If you would be considered a small client—which usually means, from a planner's perspective, that your net worth and/or income is less than her average client's—you may not get the attention or treatment you would like, particularly if the planner's compensation is based on or related to the value of your assets. (Many planners charge an asset management fee, generally ranging from 0.5 to 1.5 percent of portfolio value.) If, at the other extreme, you are significantly larger than the planner's average client, this is a reason to think twice. The planner may be extremely interested in having you as a client and will work very hard not to lose you, but at the same time, she may give you the kid-glove treatment when what you really need is a cuff to the ear. (You should not seek coddling from your planner. You need to be challenged to be and do your financial best.)

- What are his long-term professional and personal goals?

CAN YOU RELATE?

Women "are looking for help in setting up processes and procedures to address wealth," according to Mindy Rosenthal, managing director of Campden Media and co-author of a study of affluent women by Wilmington Trust and Campden Media in association with Relative Solutions. Yes, we love great desserts, but we also want the recipes and to know where they should be filed.

Some questions, on the other hand, are really not worth asking:

- What is her investment performance? If the advisor is really a financial planner, she will not be managing all her clients' assets in the same way, but will take into account the individual preferences, goals, and constraints of each client. A good planner won't be able to give you one performance number for her clients. Indeed, beware the planner who claims, "I made 15 percent for my clients last year." This suggests she is either treating them all the same or is cherry-picking results.

- Can he put you in touch with existing clients from whom you can obtain references? You can certainly ask this question, and many prospective clients do, but realize that the names you will be given are likely those of clients who have been very happy with the planner. You will be getting—quite understandably—a biased sample.

A final word on obtaining financial planning advice: there's an emerging and respected branch called life planning that attempts to join the soft side of finance—namely, the emotions, fears, and dreams we all have around money—with the harder complexities involved in tax, retirement, estate, and investment planning. Planners espousing this approach have usually been trained in a structured process that seeks to discover a client's most cherished goals and translate these into a concrete plan for their realization.

CAN YOU RELATE?

"The depth and power of women's listening is often astonishing."—Judith Duerk, author of Circle of Stones.

SUGGESTED ROUTES

www.cfp.net

The Certified Financial Planner Board of Standards, Inc., awards the CFP® certification to professionals who have met examination, education, experience, and ethical requirements. This website provides information on the financial planning process as well as practical advice for consumers. It also offers a search function that can be used to determine if a given professional has been publicly sanctioned by the CFP® Board.

www.fpanet.org

The Financial Planning Association is a membership organization for financial planners. This website allows you to search for a planner by various criteria: location, compensation method, specialties, and asset minimums.

www.kinderinstitute.com

If you are interested in life planning—a distinct approach to financial planning that explores your deepest aspirations and goals—you can use this website to find a registered life planner by geographical location.

www.moneyclubs.com

Under the umbrella of the Women's Institute for Financial Education (www.WIFE.org), The Money Club website provides guidelines for creating women's financial groups and suggests agendas for discussion of money basics and financial planning strategies.

www.napfa.org

The National Association of Personal Financial Advisors is the membership organization for fee-only planners. The website features a planner search by location and specialty. Of particular interest is the capability to screen planners for their willingness to offer advice without requiring clients to put assets under management.

www.wiserwomen.org

The Women's Institute for a Secure Retirement focuses on the issues that constitute special threats and challenges (such as divorce, longevity, and caregiving) to the financial health of women with low and moderate incomes. This website serves as a portal to other government, association, and advocacy sites that provide useful facts and information.

Chapter Two

Women Have Beliefs about Money

There are probably few subjects more polarizing than money. It is a source of both worry and reassurance. It engenders love and hate. But what does money mean to you? Not to others, but to *you*? Two extreme answers come to mind:

> *Money means nothing to me.*
>
> *Money means everything to me.*

You may find yourself simultaneously attracted to and repelled by each of these two answers, not quite certain what you think, or what you *should* think.

At one time or another, you've probably been told, or have told others (very likely your children), one of the following: that money is not important, that it does not buy happiness, that you can't take it with you, or that it is the root of all evil.

Yet if having money does not necessarily bring happiness, not having money is surely a cause for misery. Without money one lacks possibilities and, often, hope. We see everywhere the transformative and beneficial power of money: it can buy education, health, beauty, comfort, memories, and peace of mind. Maybe we cannot take it with us, but it can change our lives for the better.

The reality is: Money is *anything.*

It can be transformed into anything we choose to do with it. We may feel at times that we have no choice about how we use our money, but in fact we probably have more freedom than we think. The challenge is that this freedom of choice is not actually free—it takes work and effort to make the right choices.

Before we learn how to be competent handlers of money, it is imperative that we examine our often subconscious beliefs about money.

Before we learn how to be competent handlers of money, it is imperative that we examine our often subconscious beliefs about money. These beliefs are often derived from earliest childhood and are, therefore, deeply—and usually stubbornly—held. As an advisor, I have found that an understanding of the role that money played in my clients' early lives is an input as important to their financial planning as knowing the outstanding balance on their mortgage or the asset allocation of their 401(k) account. I may dispense the best advice in the world, but it will be useless if it is unacceptable to a client because it violates or contradicts some long-held belief.

Subconscious beliefs are not unique to my clients. Even money experts have them. When I sold my share of the financial planning practice, I received proceeds sufficient to fund a comfortable retirement, assuming I invested wisely and managed my cash flow. Easy for me, right? Well, for months I kept my stash in cash. I was simply incapable of putting the money in an investment that might lose value, despite everything I knew—and preached—about the benefits of long-term investment and the ravages of inflation on uninvested assets.

What was going on here? As I thought about it, I realized that as a child, I had watched my parents put every penny, earned and borrowed, into their home, because in their day a home almost never decreased in value and was considered one of the safest investments you could make. Cash to me was what a house had been to my parents: it seemed a way to freeze what I had worked so hard to earn. For those first few months of retirement, all I had learned and practiced during my adult years was simply no match for the power of what I had believed since I was a child.

Circling In on Your Money Beliefs

Get together with your female friends for a relaxed evening to tell your own money story, what your parents did for a living, how money was handled in your household, or funny and not-so-funny money habits you acquired as a result of your upbringing.

Understanding our beliefs about money is important because these in turn direct our behavior with money, which is perhaps the most significant factor in determining whether or not we become financially successful. We need to be aware that decisions about money often are not rational choices, but rather emotional responses born of early experience. To be financially successful, we have to make fewer irrational and impulsive decisions derived from emotional responses, and more rational and deliberate choices.

Both rational and irrational decisions can be subdivided into long-term and short-term ones. Possible financial choices can, therefore, be represented by the following Money Actions Graph:

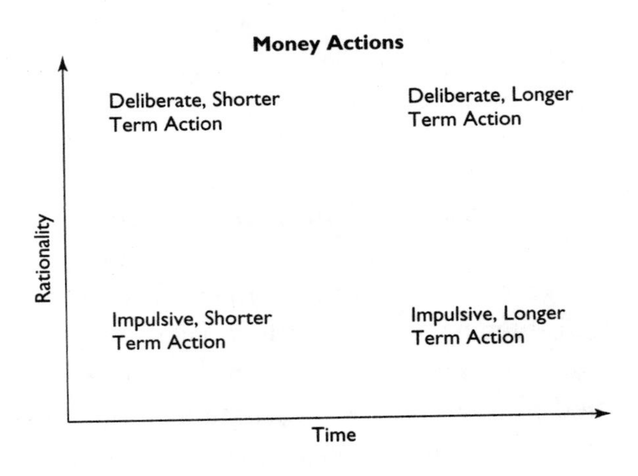

EXERCISE 2–1. WHAT DO YOU BELIEVE ABOUT MONEY?

You have likely done this in your mind if you've ever bought a lottery ticket. Imagine a sum about five or six times your annual income (or what you think your annual income should be) and assume that I just handed you a tax-free check for that amount. Take no more than three minutes—first thoughts are important—to write down, in order of priority, six things you would do with the money. Try to set aside any ideas about what you *should* do. What do you *want* to do?

Your answers likely ranged from the sensible to the frivolous, from fulfilling long-term objectives to indulgent whims. Consider the very first thing on your list. Does this tell you something important about what you believe money is for?

There are generally four ways in which we use money:

- Spending
- Purchasing
- Hoarding
- Investing

Relating these uses to the Money Actions Graph above, our new graph would look like this:

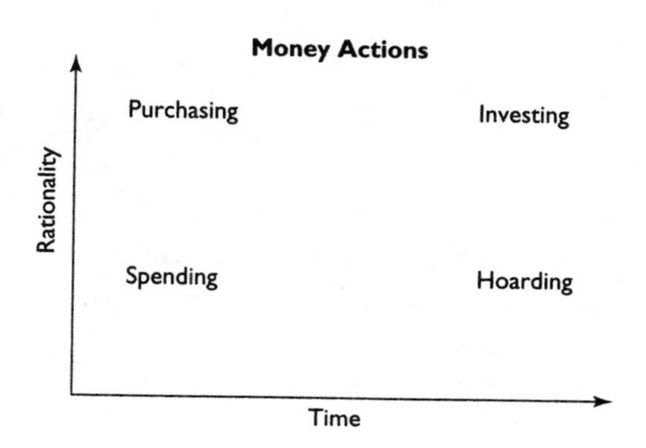

Let's consider each of these activities and the kinds of beliefs that underlie them.

Spending

This word is often used in the context of buying everyday, inexpensive items without much forethought. Since women are often responsible for fulfilling the daily needs of a household, most of us engage in this activity when buying food or other necessities. However, we also spend as a form of recreation or entertainment. Have an afternoon free? Let's go shopping! And off we go buying products and brands we did not even know we wanted until we were told we did by a multibillion-dollar marketing industry.

Purchasing

The activity of purchasing may seem similar to spending, but the formality of the word alerts us to a difference. We usually talk about purchasing when buying big or important things: homes, cars, or life insurance policies. I have never talked about purchasing a bag of Doritos. There is a deliberateness—an underlying rational process—that motivates purchasing.

Hoarding

Hoarding involves keeping something of perceived value for a very long time. It stands in contrast to spending in the sense that it involves holding onto something as opposed to letting it go. When we think of famous hoarders, George Eliot's Silas Marner comes to mind. He was a greedy man fascinated with gold—a tangible form of wealth that seems even more concrete, solid, and safe than money.

Investing

Investing is a long-term use for money and requires careful, rational consideration. No doubt some investments are made impulsively, but arguably the investor in that case is more of a purchaser or even a spender, buying an attractive idea without careful review of what she is getting.

Using some real-life examples of what women do with their money, the more detailed Money Actions Graph might look like this:

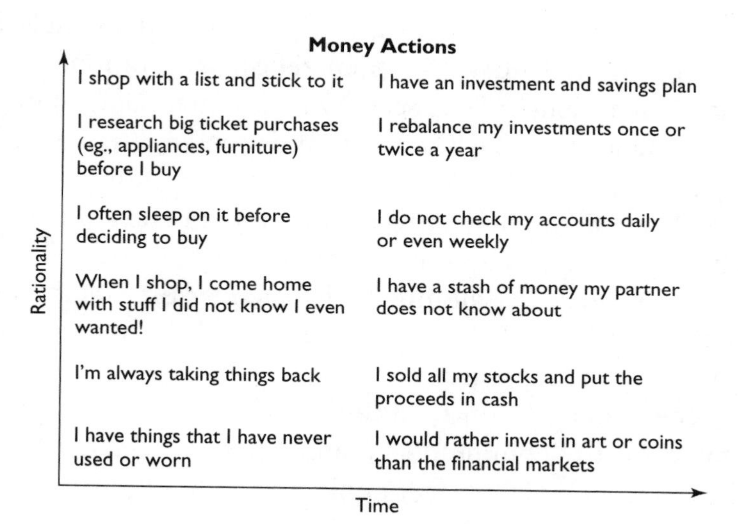

EXERCISE 2–2. WHAT DO YOUR MONEY ACTIONS LOOK LIKE?

Let's return to the list of six things you would do with more money. Of the uses for the money you listed, can any or all of them be mapped into one of the four money actions quadrants we discussed above? Can you relate these uses to any examples of money handling you learned as a child? Are there any financial choices (and beliefs) you would like to change? And for those of you who are parents, have you observed your children handling money in a way that reflects one of these beliefs?

Although many factors are at play in financial decisions, both spending and hoarding often reflect an irrational fear of scarcity.

Although many factors are at play in financial decisions, both spending and hoarding often reflect an irrational fear of scarcity. That a spender fears scarcity may at first seem counterintuitive. We talk about "big spenders" and their apparent belief that money is inexhaustible. However, for many, spending is actually an act of acquisition, of locking in something that is perceived to be valuable but that may not be available tomorrow. Where the hoarder may gloat, "It's all mine!" the spender may be motivated by the thought "It's not all mine, but it will be!" Each is an expression of worries about scarcity.

The inherent contradiction in the spending impulse is illustrated by a telephone discussion I had with my sister during the dot-com stock market bubble. She was complaining that her husband's investments—mostly in hi-tech companies—were tanking. I was about to give her the batten-down-the-hatches-and-eliminate-all-unnecessary-spending speech when she said something that completely baffled me. She said she was really sorry she had not used some of the investment money to buy a new living room sofa. "At least that way," she said, "I would still have the sofa." I realized then that she saw spending as a way of holding on to value that was constantly at risk in the stock market.

Purchasing and investing involve a careful and thoughtful approach to money that ensures there is a sufficient amount to meet our needs, both for the short term and in the future. We have a very clear idea of our goals and use money, not as an end in itself, but as a means to achieve those ends. This is not to say that all spending and hoarding activities have to be eliminated from our lives. Getting and treasuring stuff—other ways of expressing what we do when we spend or hoard—can be fun and pleasurable. Nor is all spending and hoarding irrational. In fact, in Chapter 5, I discuss the benefits of deliberate and purposeful spending. Spending and hoarding belong in our lives, but our lives cannot belong to them.

A good example of how rational thinking should replace emotional reactions occurred during the bear market of 2000. Stocks were falling and would fall over the next two years; from March 2000 to October 2002, the S&P 500 fell by 50 percent and the NASDAQ dropped by even more: 80 percent. My clients were deeply discouraged and lived in constant fear of greater losses of that scarce resource: money. My advice to them, however, was not to pull their investments and hoard whatever was left, but to cut their spending as much as possible. It was the one way they could maintain some financial control without sacrificing their rational long-term goals.

Let us go back to the very first question posed in this section: What does money mean to you? In addition to the previous answers, *nothing* and *everything*, I propose another:

It's just grease.

The new option—the idea that money is just grease—is the one I encourage you to consider as we go forward on this journey of financial discovery. Thinking of money as just grease is a great way to put it in its proper perspective. It does not do anything on its own, but properly used with foresight and reason, it makes things happen, makes things *go*. By itself, it is a toxic substance and can be very messy. Applied sensibly on a routine basis, it can make life run more smoothly.

SUGGESTED ROUTES

Black, Hilary, ed. *The Secret Currency of Love: The Unabashed Truth about Women, Money, and Relationships*, William Morrow, 2009.

Mellan, Olivia, and Sherry Christie. *Money Shy to Money Sure: A Woman's Road Map to Financial Well-Being*, Walker & Company, 2001.

Perle, Liz. *Money, A Memoir: Women, Emotions, and Cash*, Henry Holt and Company, 2006.

Chapter Three

Women Have Worth

How many times do we think back to our twenties—a time when perhaps we were newlyweds or graduate students or had just left home for our first real jobs and apartments—with a sense of wistfulness or fondness? Why do we so often call these times "the good old days"? Perhaps because things were simpler then. Ironically, this was largely because we had very little money. As a result, we had few choices and few decisions to make. Decision-making was a luxury we couldn't afford. We simply made do.

As we mature and become more established in our jobs, we generally earn more. We also often begin to worry more. The more money we have, the more choices we have, and the more decisions we have to make. Should I renovate the kitchen before I sell my house? Should I obtain travel insurance for my trip to Europe? Should I send my child to private school so she can get into a better college? Should I help my sister with a gift or a loan? We often think of the wealthy as people who don't have to worry about money, but in fact it is the wealthy who are constantly confronted with difficult choices about money—and these choices are rarely clearly right or wrong.

I have noticed, both in myself and in my female clients, that too often the way we deal with these tricky financial decisions is to avoid them. The most basic example is that we frequently pay exactly what we are asked to pay. When I am hired to do a financial plan, I give clients the price of the plan and tell them they can pay a certain portion upfront with the balance to be billed later. Almost invariably, women will make out a check for the full amount. Many men, on the other hand, defer payment altogether for a few days while they think about it. They usually end up retaining me, but are in no hurry to pay. They withhold payment as a negotiation tactic. Sometimes they even come back and try to lower the fee. It seems like my women clients want to get the decision to hire me over with, whereas the men don't mind spending some time weighing up the pros and cons.

Managing your finances is like managing your health. You cannot not be involved.

Our female fear of making financial decisions keeps us from controlling our money and this failure to control, in turn, keeps us fearful. It's a pernicious cycle that usually leads women to leave financial decisions to someone else—their spouse, partner, accountant, bank, even the IRS. Managing your finances, however, is like managing your health. You cannot *not* be involved. While you can delegate some decision-making, you cannot abdicate your responsibility to ensure those decisions are right for you.

The only way to break the cycle is to gain knowledge, and the first step in gaining financial knowledge is finding out what you're worth, or what you have. In the financial world, these are termed your *assets*. The second—and more important—step is knowing what you want, often referred to as your financial goals.

WHAT DO YOU HAVE? YOUR ASSETS

Financial assets are things (although they need not be limited to things, as we will see in the next chapter) with economic value. They are commonly classified using the following four characteristics.

Maturity: Short-term or long-term

Short-term assets are intended or available for use within a year or less. Cash holdings are generally considered short-term assets, however, not because they definitely will be used in a year, but because they can be. Retirement accounts, on the other hand, are usually thought to be long-term, even if they are currently being used or are in cash, because retirement happens over many years.

Use: Personal, investment, or business

Our home is considered a personal use asset, whereas property we rent out is generally classified as an investment property. Business assets include closely held and managed companies, or assets used within those companies.

Tax treatment: Qualified or non-qualified

Qualified refers to the special tax treatment accorded to investments held in employer-sponsored or individual retirement plans. They are generally not taxed until they are withdrawn from the retirement plan. *Non-qualified* holdings, on the other hand, are assets that are taxed either on an ongoing basis as they earn income or on the capital gain if the asset is sold before death.

Security type: Fixed income or equity

This asset classification is based on the way in which our money is put to work. Put in its simplest terms, if we lend money to a company, we own fixed-income assets or bonds. If we buy part of the company, we own equity or stocks.

These categories are not mutually exclusive. For example, your business may hold a one-year certificate of deposit that would simultaneously qualify as a short-term, fixed-income asset for business use.

As you can see, the classification of assets quickly gets very technical. For now, it is enough to have heard of these various classifications should they come up in future financial discussions.

EXERCISE 3–1. DO YOU KNOW WHAT YOU HAVE AND DON'T HAVE?

Take two sheets of paper. Write the title "What I Have" on the first sheet and list all your financial resources. Write the title "What I Don't Have" on the second sheet and list everything you are financially lacking.

Now step back and review your lists. What's first on your "What I Have" list? Any ideas why it is first? Is it something important to you? Most used? Most available? Most worried about? Why? Do you believe that the list is complete? Did you include your human capital (i.e., your earning potential over your lifetime) on the list? Did you include values for your assets? If not, do you know what they are?

What's first on your "What I Don't Have" list? Any ideas why it is first? Have you listed things you really need? Have you listed things you want? Have you listed things that other people have that you want? Have you listed things that other people have that you don't want? Can this list be used in any way to define or refine your financial goals?

This exercise should tell you a lot about the level of your engagement with your assets and how you view them. Your answers should establish whether you know where you are and where you would (and would not) like to go. If you had difficulty with the first list, this might indicate that you need more information about your assets. If you had difficulty with the second you may need to think about or rethink your financial objectives.

You may recognize the first list as an initial attempt at preparing what financial experts call a balance sheet or personal financial statement. A balance sheet also lists liabilities or debts. Subtracting the value of your liabilities (what you owe) from the value of your assets (what you have) provides the measure of your net worth. Many people consider net worth to be extremely important to financial planning; the bigger the number, the more financially successful you are deemed to be. The truth is that your financial success depends far less on what you have and much more on what you do with what you have.

Now let's get more specific.

EXERCISE 3–2. HOW MUCH DO YOU KNOW ABOUT YOUR ASSETS?

Set aside a piece of paper for every asset you own. Ten assets = ten pieces of paper. You can also save paper by creating your sheets online.

For each asset, fill in the following information:

What do I/we have? ____________________

Who owns it? ____________________
(e.g., is it in my name,
in my partner's name, joint,
tenants-in-common?)

Did I/we borrow to get it? ____________________

How much did I/we borrow? ____________________

When did I/we borrow? ____________________

For how long? ____________________

What is the rate?	________________
Who manages it?	________________
What are the costs?	________________
Who gets it after me?	________________
Do I understand it? (e.g., how it performs)	________________
Can I easily use it or change it?	________________
What is its value?	________________
WHAT IS IT FOR?	________________

Here's an example of what your answers might look like.

What do I/we have?	Our house
Who owns it? (is it in my name, in my partner's name, joint, tenants-in-common?)	Joint, I think
Did I/we borrow to get it?	Yes
How much did I/we borrow?	$300,000
When did I/we borrow?	April 2005
For how long?	30 years
What is the rate?	6%
Who manages it?	I do
What are the costs?	Not sure; real estate taxes are $4,500
Who gets it after me?	My kids, I hope

Do I understand it? (e.g., how it performs)	Not sure
Can I easily use it or change it?	Would be hard to sell right now, but I can get a home equity line if I needed to
What is its value?	$500,000 (?)
WHAT IS IT FOR?	What does this mean?

You may have a hard time coming up with all the answers. Knowing the terms of your loans or the titling on your assets might require some digging or rummaging through file drawers. You may even be so discouraged that you think, "I hate this stuff. I don't have time. *This* is why I don't like finances." Try replacing these thoughts with, "This stuff is my life. I love my life and what I can do with it. I will find the time. I am worth it!"

WHAT IS IT FOR? YOUR VALUES

Mastering this information is something that cannot, repeat *cannot*, be delegated. I tell you this as a professional to whom clients come thinking that one of my skill sets includes divining the amount of cash value on their life insurance from the look in their eyes. There is no easy way to collect this crucial information. There are no shortcuts. Obtaining the details generally involves gathering statements and recent tax returns and/or getting on the phone to financial providers and asking them to provide this information. Try not to become overwhelmed. Take this one step at a time.

What values are most important to you in life? Only by discerning these can you properly establish your financial goals.

Now let us consider another, equally important question: what are your assets for? To answer this question you need to consider your values. I am not talking here about asset values, but values that are even more crucial to a comprehensive financial plan, namely your own personal, non-dollar-dominated values. What values are most important to you in life? Only by discerning these can you properly establish your financial goals. These are the ends to which our assets are ultimately the means.

EXERCISE 3–3. WHAT ARE YOUR PERSONAL VALUES?

Consider the following personal values and circle the ones most meaningful to you:

Creativity/personal expression

Professional development

Growth (of self)

Growth (of others)

Family

Relationships

Health (physical, mental, and/or spiritual)

Independence/autonomy

Personal legacy

Sense of control

Security

Enjoyment/fun

(Add others that pertain to you.)

EXERCISE 3–4. WHAT DOES YOUR VALUE PORTFOLIO LOOK LIKE?

Consider the values that you circled in Exercise 3–3 as components of your own personal portfolio of what is most important to you. Draw a circle (a pie) to represent this personal portfolio of values, and divide the pie into segments representing each of your values (see below for an example). The larger the segment, the more important the value is in your portfolio. (Using a pie chart for such intangibles as values is an idea from David Corbett, author of *Portfolio Life: The New Path to Work, Purpose, and Passion After 50.*)

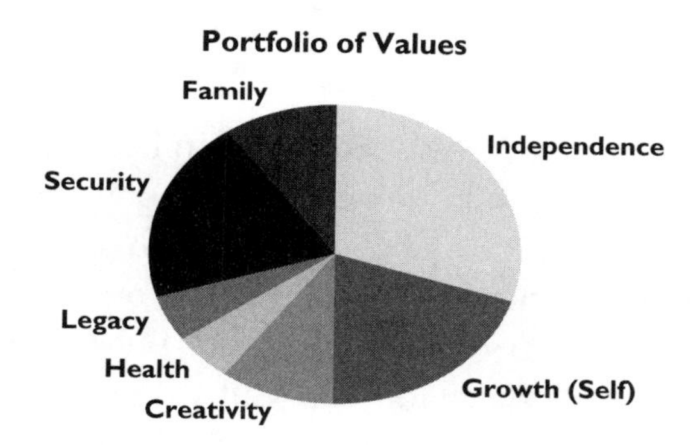

You may find the allocation of your values difficult. Your indecision about what you value may have resulted in a pie divided into as many equal segments as you have values. If so, try the following exercise to gain a clearer sense of what really is most important to you.

EXERCISE 3–5. PRIORTIZING YOUR VALUES

Choose two values you have given equal weight to that seem to involve a trade-off: more of one will mean less of the other. For example, you may simultaneously cherish your family and value your independence; the two values frequently vie for your time and attention. Now make the following assumption. You are given an extra day each week. The rest of the world goes along as usual with seven days, but you get an extra day to spend exactly as you choose. Let's assume, not unrealistically, that you will spend your bonus time doing things you most value. Take the pair of values you identified above, which were initially equal in priority, and allocate the sixteen waking hours of your extra day between those two values. Having this additional unconstrained time often frees us to reveal our preferences. We can give more to one value without feeling like we are taking away from another. Continue with other similar pairings of your values to get a better sense of how your personal pie would be allocated.

EXERCISE 3–6. HOW DO YOU VALUE YOUR ASSETS?

Now go back to the asset sheets you created in Exercise 3–2. In the space next to "What is it for?" try to write in one or two of your values for each asset. This may be difficult. At this point, you may not see an obvious connection between what you value and what you have. If there seems to be no relationship, put a question mark in the "What is it for?" space for now. But where it is possible to assign personal values to your assets, go ahead. You may have, for example, a small savings account that has just been sitting there. Based on your values pie, you may see how important your professional development is to you. Accordingly, you might now begin to see your savings account as having value as a fund for your career growth—to take some courses, perhaps, or to tide you over while you look for another, better job.

The purpose of this exercise should now be obvious: your primary objective is to create a better alignment between your resources and what is most important to you. This cannot happen immediately, of course. What you have needs to grow, and in some cases be rearranged, to bring your financial worth in harmony with your self-worth.

Circling In on Financial Goals

You may want to form a small circle—perhaps you and one or two trusted friends—to help you set financial goals, both short- and long-term. Use their help to keep these goals S.M.A.R.T.: Specific, Measurable, Achievable, Realistic, and Time-bound. This circle would also be a good place to share your portfolio of values—how you would like your time, effort, and money allocated to the things you most strongly believe in.

PROTECT WHAT YOU HAVE: INSURANCE

In my *Random House Webster's Unabridged Dictionary*, the words *worth* and *worry* are on the same page. This is as it should be.

No sooner do we acquire worth than we begin to worry about losing it. Therefore, no discussion about making the proper use of your assets is complete without an overview of how to protect yourself from losing them. This requires a brief summary of the kinds of insurance available and the best way to obtain these coverages.

Studies show that most women are worriers, so you would think we would be the first to educate ourselves about insurance as a way to protect ourselves from life's uncertainties: loss of health, premature death, or loss of property (see Table 3.1). But there is ample evidence that women are not smart insurance consumers. For example, our spouses are much more likely to carry life insurance than we are. Many women are unaware that their need for disability insurance is much greater than their husband's.

So how do you purchase the best policy for you at a price you can afford? Insurance is a minefield of fine print. If ever there were devils in details, they are in the contractual language of multi-page insurance policies. I strongly recommend that you consult with a specialist to help you compare, in simpler language, the features of various policies and the costs and benefits of each. You have to be sure you are getting what you need, not paying unnecessarily for what you don't need.

The ideal specialist would be an independent insurance broker who is not captive to one insurance company and who acts in your interest. When interviewing or hiring such a specialist, ask whether in addition to finding the appropriate policies for you, she or he can also represent you when you have a claim or a dispute with an insurer.

Insurance should not be considered as an investment or a way to pay routine bills.

Table 3.1. Insurance Options.

If you have ...	you need ...	because ...
Children or other dependents	Life insurance on yourself	Others rely on your financial support and/or caretaking.
A partner, a spouse, or an ex-spouse	Life insurance on him/her	You depend on his/her financial support.
An income	Disability insurance on yourself	You cannot afford the loss of income in the event you cannot work.
A partner or spouse with income	Disability insurance on your partner or spouse	You cannot afford the loss of another's income in the event he/she cannot work.
A home	Homeowner's insurance	You won't be able to get a mortgage without it. You cannot afford to replace or repair your home in the event of a loss.
Valuable personal possessions	Renter's or homeowner's insurance	You cannot afford to replace your personal property in the event it is destroyed or stolen.

(continued)

Table 3.1. *(continued)*

If you have ...	you need ...	because ...
An auto	Car insurance	You won't be able to get a car loan without it. In most states, you cannot drive legally without it. You cannot afford to replace or repair your car if it is in an accident. You cannot afford to pay for others' loss of health, life, or property in the event of an accident.
Your health	Medical insurance	You cannot afford the health care costs of a catastrophic disease, accident, or illness.
Assets you wish to protect in retirement or for your children	Long-term care insurance	You cannot afford the costs of prolonged nursing care.
Substantial net worth, a business, or your reputation	Excess liability coverage; errors and omissions insurance	You cannot afford the possible damages of a lawsuit against you.

Here are some general rules for becoming a smart purchaser of insurance to protect your worth:

- Insure *only* what you cannot afford to lose. (Notice that in Table 3.1, the reason for just about every type of coverage started with the words: "You cannot afford . . .")

- Recognize that emotional loss is not the same as financial loss. You should insure only the latter.

- Keep your focus on the loss protection provided by any given insurance coverage, and not on other, often extraneous benefits. Insurance should not be considered as an investment or a way to pay routine bills.

Some corollaries of these rules are as follows:

- Don't bother to insure what to you would be a small loss, and keep the deductibles on your policies as high as possible. Same goes for elimination periods, which are similar to deductibles in that they define a period of time before your insurance coverage takes effect. By extending your elimination period, you can usually reduce the cost of your premium.

- Don't insure the lives of children or overinsure the life of your husband or partner just because you would be devastated to lose them.

- Don't insure personal items that are priceless only to you personally.

- Don't get too fancy, narrow, or overspecialized when it comes to insurance. Forget about accidental death and dismemberment policies (unless they are free, as may be the case at your workplace), or policies that cover quirky events, such as loss of sight in your right eye *and* loss of use of your left foot, or loss of *all* your credit cards. I'd even think twice about travel insurance that covers the cost of a canceled trip due to terrorism or illness. I would also think long and hard about any type of insurance that seems newfangled, such as insurance on loss of your identity. Yes, it is a pain in the proverbial posterior to lose your identity, but there are so many simple (and less costly) good housekeeping rules we can implement to reduce the risk of such an event (e.g., buy a shredder).

Consider long-term care insurance

One type of insurance deserves special emphasis: namely, long-term care insurance. Women generally live longer than men, and as a result they often suffer a higher incidence of chronic ailments. They also are more likely to live alone in their elderly years, and they are having fewer children who might provide needed support. This is probably why long-term care insurance is of such intense interest to my female clients. To give you a better idea as to whether or not you need this type of coverage, consider the following.

A person whose retirement income is more than $100,000 per year may not require long-term care insurance. Long-term care costs run between $80,000 to $100,000 per person per year, so this individual likely can afford the necessary care, assuming she does not have large fixed expenses, such as a mortgage or other debt, that would not go away even if she needs nursing care. (A more complicated scenario would be a couple whose retirement income is, say, $150,000 per annum. If only one of them were to get sick, it would mean trying to finance two separate lifestyles, which could cost considerably more than a joint lifestyle. To determine whether they should get coverage, they must, therefore, determine whether they can afford the additional cost.)

At the other extreme, a person who is financially destitute upon retirement does not require long-term care coverage either.

If she gets sick or disabled, her nursing home needs are likely to be covered by Medicaid, an insurance program funded by the federal and state governments and administered by the states. There is a whole branch of financial planning dedicated to Medicaid eligibility planning, which involves transferring assets or setting up trusts to accelerate the descent to financial rock bottom to qualify for assistance. Personally, I have never chosen to acquire this expertise, believing that planning to be poor for the purpose of government assistance is unethical, not to mention just plain poor financial management.

For the majority of retirees who fall between these two extremes—having resources that could easily absorb the costs of long-term care or having nothing—long-term care insurance should be seriously considered. Even those who can afford to pay the costs of long-term care may wish to consider this coverage if they don't want to unnecessarily deplete the estate they leave their children. They should, however, consider having their children pay the premiums. In the same vein, you might consider buying this insurance coverage for your parents, or other fond, rich relatives, who may be including you in their estate plans. Even for those of us who might be able to afford the costs of long-term care out of our own pockets, purchasing this insurance can be a way of maintaining our autonomy by preventing our children from feeling obligated or financially motivated to take care of us in their own homes.

Unfortunately, the reality is that those most in need of this coverage are most likely to be turned down. A variety of chronic conditions, such as arthritis or depression (or even being too old), can prevent you from obtaining this insurance. Only the government and some private employers offer employee group coverage for which eligibility is not a problem. For the rest of us, it is crucial that we turn our minds to obtaining this insurance as soon as possible, before it's too late.

Decision Point ***Should I be thinking about my financial planning separately from my spouse or partner?***

> *The answer is an unequivocal yes. This does not mean you should disregard your partner or forgo joint financial planning. It means you should think about your financial affairs as if you will be on your own at some point in your life.*

As women, we tend to want to be cared for. We all hope and dream that our intimate relationships will last as long as we do. In an article entitled "Why Retirement Is Different for Women" posted on www.bankrate.com, Sheyna Steiner quotes CFP® professional Nancy Gardner:

> . . . a significant portion of married women of all ages cede control of their financial future to their husbands. "They find finances boring," she says, "so they just let their husbands handle it." Single women of all ages also take an avoidant and slightly delusional approach, she says. "They think that they will never have the money to retire, so they don't want to think about it. I have actually had people tell me when I ask what their retirement plan is, and they tell me in all seriousness, 'Marry well.' And that is all age categories. It is really sad."

Being cared for is different from being taken care of. Sometimes we confuse the two: in seeking the first, we think we will get the second. In getting the second, we think we have a guarantee of the first. In my opinion, women's fears about becoming bag ladies may be less about running out of money than about running out of love.

The reality is this: whether women are in good, long-term relationships or not, they will almost certainly be alone at some point in their lives. Divorce is a modern-day reality. In a study released in 2002, the National Center for Health Statistics found that 20 percent of couples are divorced or separated within the first five years of marriage, and 30 percent within the first ten years.

Another reality is that women live more than five years longer than men. Even when we are living with someone, legal and familial realities often keep us financially apart. For example, in most states lesbian partners do not have the same benefits of financial merger as married couples. Many of us are in second or even third marriages, but have financial obligations and interests from earlier periods of our lives that cannot or should not be combined with those of our current spouse.

The transition from couplehood to singlehood is rarely gentle and never simple. It is almost always a time of difficult, even violent, emotions. It's hard to think, even to breathe sometimes, let alone make decisions about finances. But money issues loom large when you become single again: What's mine? What's not? Where will my money come from? Whom can I trust? What needs to be done/changed/closed/opened/paid?

The best time for planning to be single is when you are not.

The best time for planning to be single is when you are not. Think of it as a form of insurance, contingency planning, or emergency preparedness. Set aside the money now that you might need in the first several months of being single, just as you might stock up for a natural disaster on bottled water, duct tape, and canned goods. Create a phone list of the people—a CFP® professional, accountant, attorney—who can help reorient you in your new financial situation. If you have a planner now, ask her or him to prepare some what-if scenarios addressing your financial situation in the event of divorce or the death of your partner.

All of this makes perfect sense. If we haven't done it, we certainly know we should. More problematic, however, is the question of whether we should maintain a separate financial identity when we are in a relationship.

A surprising number of women keep a stash of money that their spouses or partners know nothing about. They do not see this as deceptive or an act of financial infidelity (although they are likely to be upset, even outraged, if they were to discover their significant other had a secret account of his own). For many women, having this money seems almost an act of affirmative action, a way of establishing financial parity. It is a way of catching up to the financial autonomy or independence they perceive their partners to have.

When I got married thirty-five years ago, I was in my early twenties and did not have anything of financial value either to share with my husband or to keep separate. It was exciting, and one of the customary first declarations of wedlock, to open up a joint checking account as the only household bank account. Today, however, young women are more apt to have their own careers, savings, and brokerage accounts before they marry, and may be reluctant to merge their resources with those of a partner. Household expenses are often run through three ledgers—His, Hers, and Ours—and at the end of the month she writes a check to him, or he to her, to settle the accounts. At tax time, too, these modern-day couples file their taxes jointly, but nevertheless attempt to divvy up the refunds or taxes according to their separate and disproportionate incomes or deductions.

In my experience, there is such a thing as being too financially separate in a relationship.

In my experience, there is such a thing as being too financially separate in a relationship. Even though I wholeheartedly advocate a woman having her own checking account and assets, being in a relationship entails some amount of financial merger where the lines between who contributes or spends should be erased.

CAN YOU RELATE?

"Men tend to define wealth in terms of status and power. Women see wealth equaling personal productivity and as a means to independence and empowerment, not power."—Cindy Conway, director of marketing for Wilmington Trust's Wealth Advisory Service, Investment News, May 31, 2009.

I worked with one young couple who were compatible in just about every respect, with one major exception: she liked to spend and he liked to save. They were planning to have kids and buy a larger house in a family-friendly neighborhood in the next few years. The problem was that every time she was a bit extravagant with family gifts or spa treatments, he got angry about being the only one doing the saving for their home. Our solution—which was actually more cosmetic than real—was to open a joint account into which they deposited their (unequal) paychecks. Out of this account came all household and joint goal expenses, including the eventual down payment for the house. Whatever was left over after these joint expenses were paid was then divided between them and deposited into their separate accounts. (This couple divided the residue 50/50, but in a case where a couple's income is substantially unequal, a different division might be considered.) Each was free to do with their share what he or she wished. He might do more saving, and she could spend. Because the house goal was already jointly funded, neither had any reason to question the other's choices with the money that remained.

I also recommend that couples see their financial planner together as well as separately. After a couple's session, schedule another meeting just for you. This way you can feel free to express your financial goals, preferences, and issues from your own perspective. I stress that this is not about going behind your partner's back. (Indeed, if the planner suspects that you and your partner have a true conflict of interests, she or he should identify it as such and find ways for resolution before continuing with your planning.) What you want to establish in such a one-on-one meeting is your financial identity—how you think about finances, and the way you wish to be addressed and involved by your planner. Some planners have a tendency to think of a couple as one client, but they should keep in mind that a couple is a team of two individuals trying to work toward common financial goals. The distinction is subtle, but important.

CAN YOU RELATE?

Too often, when it comes to identifying our values, women let others make that determination. There is an old aphorism: "A man will pay $2 for a $1 *item that he really wants. A woman will pay $1 for a $2 item that she does not really want." There is some painful truth to this. Women's perception of their values frequently comes from others. The most crucial step to proper financial planning, therefore, is to determine what your personal values really are.*

SUGGESTED ROUTES

http://iasp.brandeis.edu/womenandaging/finance
The National Program on Women and Aging website provides links to financial planning resources for women, including sites where you will find financial calculators.

www.lawdepot.com
LawDepot.com is an online legal contract service with an option for compiling your balance sheet in a format commonly required by banks, lenders, and investors.

www.mint.com
Mint.com is a popular virtual file cabinet for consolidating and updating all your financial information. You enter information on bank, investment, credit card, and loan accounts, which is then updated each time you log on, to give you a bird's-eye view of your net worth and cash flow status. Based on your account transactions, Mint also alerts you to possible savings you can realize by switching to other financial providers or services.

www.quicken.intuit.com
Quicken offers a free online or subscription program that helps track your banking and investment accounts and can be used for budgeting and expense management.

www.sewallbelmont.org
Though not a financial resource, Sewall–Belmont's site nevertheless provides a source of inspiration and information for women asserting their worth. An historic home in Washington, DC, Sewall–Belmont House is the headquarters of the National Women's Party and now sponsors programs and initiatives celebrating the equality and leadership of women in a number of areas, such as business, politics, and finance.

Armstrong, Alexandra, & Mary R. Donahue, "On Your Own: A Widow's Passage to Emotional and Financial Well-Being" Armstrong, Fleming, & Moore, 2006.

Chapter Four

Women Work—Maximizing Your Human Capital

So far we have talked about assets as things: accounts, personal property, homes. As discussed in the previous chapter, a common definition of an asset is any item of value. But, in fact, our most valuable asset is not a thing or possession at all, and is never included on conventionally prepared balance sheets or statements of net worth. It is our ability to turn our intelligence, education, skills, and experience into income through work. In short, our most valuable asset is our human capital.

For most of us, our human capital is the primary means to wealth.

For most of us, our human capital is the primary means to wealth. A few of us get wealthy through an inheritance, and fewer still win the lottery, and while we may daydream of such windfalls, all too often they bring unhappiness or dislocation to our lives. The popular media has us believing that wealth is just one hot investment tip away, but, in reality, significant wealth is seldom created through investments in stocks, bonds, and other traditional assets. It can be preserved and gently grown via these means, but it usually takes training, hard work, and discipline, and sometimes a great idea to become wealthy.

A while ago I was asked by the editor of my college alumnae quarterly to do a "money makeover" for a much younger alumna. But when the editor gave me the particulars of my subject, I began to have reservations. She was twenty-eight years old, renting an apartment, had no savings, an income of $25,000 a year, and $10,000 in credit card and student loan debt. In other words, she was totally unlike the affluent, midlife client I generally advise. Without assets, there was apparently very little to make over. As I met and got to know my charge, however, it became clear that while she had very few assets, her human capital potential was huge.

My makeover subject had more clarity of purpose and determination to reach her goals than just about anyone I had ever counseled. She had a master's degree in public administration and wanted to go back to get an MBA. She wanted to set up a business to import the wares of working mothers in her native Bangladesh. She had grace, confidence, enthusiasm, and enormous gratitude for the few crumbs of basic financial advice I was able to give her. After one telephone interview, I knew I was talking to a potentially successful and wealthy woman.

Women often perceive that not asking for what they are worth is a necessary trade-off for being allowed to keep their job when they take maternity leave, or to leave early or work from home to take care of a child.

It must be said, however, that discrimination, both real and perceived, still exists in the workplace to keep women's earnings lower than men's, and prevents women from attaining the same promotions and advancements. Much of this is related to what social scientists call women's "reduced workforce attachment." Many drop out of the workforce, either temporarily or permanently, usually to take care of children or other dependents. It is not only the time off that causes women to fare worse economically, although the lost earnings during these periods can be significant. It is women's fear to push for more money in the substantial period *before* they take their leave to have a baby or take a parental leave that often results in a greater loss. Women often perceive that not asking for what they are worth is a necessary trade-off for being allowed to keep their job when they take maternity leave, or to leave early or work from home to take care of a child. Furthermore, upon their return from taking leave, they continue to take home less than their peers because they are often perceived as lacking job experience, or training, or seniority—or employers eye them with suspicion because they may leave again.

The news is not all bad, of course, and positive changes are taking place. The pay gap is not as wide at upper levels of management, and more women are breaking through the glass ceiling to these executive positions. But the changes are happening slowly, and a truly gender-neutral working world will take time to evolve. In view of this reality, it is even more crucial for women than men to manage and maximize their human capital. This may not result in complete earnings parity with men, but women who pay attention to growing this asset can improve their situation significantly.

VALUING YOUR HUMAN CAPITAL

So what are our skills and experience worth in the marketplace? Since we are looking at earning potential as an asset, we will be applying the same concepts used when discussing ways to maximize the income or gain potential of other assets, namely value, risk, and return. A near-universal principle in the world of asset management is that we want the maximum return from our assets while taking on an acceptable level of risk. Our goals with respect to our earnings are no different: we are trying to get more out of ourselves without unnecessary risk.

Since value is the price that brings a willing buyer and seller together, the value of your productive capacity can be obtained by finding out what employers are willing to pay for your or similar qualifications.

Since value is the price that brings a willing buyer and seller together, the value of your productive capacity can be obtained by finding out what employers are willing to pay for your or similar qualifications. Not long ago, the way to gather information about how we stacked up relative to our peers was around the water cooler. Employees always seemed to get the whisper on what their colleagues are making, no matter how determined employers are about keeping such information confidential. But we now have much more accurate, less hush-and-tell means at our disposal.

The Department of Labor's *Occupational Outlook Handbook* is a good place to start. Available online or in hard copy, it is issued every two years and provides, by state, job market data under various headings, including required training and education, potential earnings, responsibilities, work environment for specific jobs, and so on. Job-seeking websites like www.monster.com also have career benchmarking tools to help you determine whether you are above or below your professional peers. The human resource section on www.payscale.com also contains compensation and job analysis tools.

Another way to help you establish your worth is to learn more about your employer. Do you know the budget for your company or its profitability? What are the staff metrics used to assess company performance? In my profession, for example, some common measures are revenue per employee, clients per employee, and assets-under-management per employee. How does your job contribute, if at all, to your company's performance? Understanding where you fit in to the company's overall financial success may not tell you your worth directly, but it will give you an indicator. It will also give you a sense of your leverage when it comes to asking for a salary or wage increase or a promotion.

If you are self-employed, of course, you are dependent on what the marketplace will pay for your goods or services. This is determined by many different factors, many of which you may not have any control over. Nevertheless, in my experience, one of the primary ways that self-employed women—especially those who provide services rather than goods—tend to discount their value is by undercharging. They seem to believe, with a woman's characteristic humility, that if they charge less they will keep their clients or get more business in the future. What they overlook is the ironic truth that if they charge more, they are often perceived as being worth more and, therefore, will be valued more. This is a virtuous cycle that many female business owners would do well to tap into.

EXERCISE 4–1. HOW MUCH IS YOUR HUMAN CAPITAL WORTH?

Let's suppose that, as a result of your research, you have determined your current value in the workplace expressed as an annual wage. We are now going to turn that annual value into one you can list with the other assets on your balance sheet. Using a spreadsheet program, such as Microsoft Excel or Macintosh iWork Numbers, or just a piece of paper, project your earnings over a given period of time (see Table 4.1). This period can correspond to your working life or a shorter period of your choosing. However, I recommend using as long a time period as possible, both because our working lives—even if interrupted—are very long and because taking a long-term view will show you just how large an asset your human capital can be.

In adding your earnings, take into account a reasonable growth rate to reflect cost-of-living and, if applicable, merit increases. The example below assumes a 2 percent annual increase. You then tally up these earnings. In the example below, a net present value (NPV) sum is computed that also takes into account a discount rate to reflect that a dollar earned in later years is worth less than a dollar earned today. The Excel formula for NPV is provided in Table 4.2.

Your discount rate (i.e., the "rate" term in the NPV formula above) can be set to the long-term rate of inflation. A good number to use is 3 percent, which reflects the historical average inflation rate. You might assume that your earnings will increase over time at a cost-of-living rate, in which case you continue to earn in real terms what you make today. In this case your total value is your annual income times the number of years in your projection period.

What you should appreciate, whatever method you use, is that the value of your earnings is by no means insignificant. It is every bit as important to grow and manage as your investment accounts.

INVEST IN YOURSELF

Now that you appreciate how important an asset you represent, how can you increase your worth?

Table 4.1. Project Your Earnings

Year	Earnings
1	______________
2	______________
3	______________
4	______________
5	______________
6	______________
7	______________
8	______________
9	______________
10	______________
.	______________
.	______________
.	______________
VALUE	______________

Table 4.2. NPV: Excel Formula

Year	Earnings
1	$ 50,000
2	$ 51,000
3	$ 52,020
4	$ 53,060
5	$ 54,122
6	$ 55,204
7	$ 56,308
8	$ 57,434
9	$ 58,583
10	$ 59,755
VALUE	$464,768

VALUE formula:
= NPV (rate, value1, value2, ...)

Women usually think that to make more we must *do* more: work harder, work longer, and/or get more training and education. There is no doubt that such efforts often pay off over our lives. Simply adding three more years of work at the end of your career, for example—a possibility many baby boomers now have to consider out of necessity—can boost your wealth considerably over your lifetime. The large bang for this relatively small buck is due to the combined effects of the following: a) having three more years to make retirement plan contributions; b) delaying social security benefits, which leads to a higher monthly benefit when you do collect; and c) avoiding three years of draw-down on retirement assets.

Another way to look at it is that, by one estimate, a fifty-seven-year-old woman looking to retire at age sixty-two with $500,000 in retirement assets can have 20 percent more spendable income at retirement if she delays her retirement for three years. Studies have also shown, for example, that a college education can increase lifetime earnings by as much as $1 million, and that delaying the birth of a child by just one year can increase a woman's wages over her career by 10 percent.

There is also a simpler step you can take, one often taken by men but seldom by women: ask for more.

But there is also a simpler step you can take, one often taken by men but seldom by women: *ask* for more. In *Women Don't Ask: Negotiation and the Gender Divide*, authors Linda Babcock and Sara Laschever estimate that 20 percent of women fail to negotiate their compensation packages—and real money is lost by this failure. One study cited by Babcock and Laschever estimates that women who consistently negotiate for a higher salary can amass up to an incredible $1 million in additional earnings over their lifetime compared with women who don't.

Teaching women how to negotiate for what they are worth is the subject of several books and websites. As a financial planner, I can state with certainty that the investment of time and money spent on improving those skills can make women wealthy in a way that simply becoming savvier about investing cannot. Invest in yourself first.

An alternative way to invest in you is to work for—and pay—yourself. There are 10.1 million woman-owned businesses in this country. Self-employment certainly is one way to address the inequities found in the workplace, and though the survival rates for businesses held by women are generally lower than those for male-owned businesses, recent data suggest that women-owned companies are growing stronger. These businesses have fared better in the recent recession than male-owned companies due to women's greater reluctance to borrow. Other sources have compared recent female unemployment to male unemployment, and have found almost 50 percent more men out of work than women. The gender difference has been significant enough to result in coinage of the term *mancession* to describe the job losses of the 2008–09 recession.

Advising women how to go into business for themselves is beyond the purview of this book, but it is worth mentioning the tremendous wealth-building possibilities for those who move in this direction. No doubt the risks are enormous, but women business owners may avoid problems of the gender wage gap or the workplace discrimination they can face when trying to balance the demands of an employer with their own family needs and caretaking requirements. I, therefore, offer encouragement to all women to at least consider this route. Indeed, in the case of entrepreneurship, women may well have at least one advantage over men: they have status as minority business owners who can borrow on preferential terms and access special government assistance.

Returning to Table 4.2, we should now add columns to project how the contingencies we have discussed can affect earnings, both negatively and positively. Below is a sample sheet that illustrates possible changes in the value of human capital resulting from a 10 percent raise, a three-year leave to have kids, and a leave to obtain specialized training.

Table 4.3. Changes in Value of Human Capital: Three Examples

Year	Earnings	What If?	What If?	What If?
		Ask for Raise	Leave for Kids	Get Retraining
1	$ 50,000	$ 55,000	$ 50,000	$ 0
2	$ 51,000	$ 56,100	$ 51,000	$ 0
3	$ 52,020	$ 57,222	$ 52,020	$ 75,000
4	$ 53,060	$ 58,366		$ 76,500
5	$ 54,122	$ 59,534		$ 78,030
6	$ 55,204	$ 60,724		$ 79,591
7	$ 56,308	$ 61,939	$ 52,020	$ 81,182
8	$ 57,434	$ 63,178	$ 53,060	$ 82,806
9	$ 58,583	$ 64,441	$ 54,122	$ 84,462
10	$ 59,755	$ 65,730	$ 55,204	$ 86,151
	$464,768	$511,245	$326,423	$530,785

As you can see, the returns—and the costs—of your workplace choices can be significant: a 10 percent increase from asking for and getting a raise in year one; a 14 percent return from an investment in your skills; and a 33 percent cost for the decision to stay at home for three years with your children.

The choice is, of course, more than a financial calculation and involves those non-monetary values emphasized in Chapter 3. The challenge is to become aware of and manage these contingencies in your working life with a view to optimizing your biggest asset. As I have discussed, you can do this yourself. Alternatively, if you seek the assistance of a financial planner, make sure she also models these contingencies in her projections. Sometimes the software used by planners or the tools available online allow only straight-line projections of income over time, and fail to take into account these ups and downs and ins and outs that are part of every woman's life.

CONSIDER THE BENEFITS

While we have so far discussed ways to grow your earnings, there is another often hidden but just as powerful way for employees to boost their human capital, namely employer benefits. The value of these benefits is evident from the fact that they can increase an employer's payroll costs by as much as 20 to 40 percent of an employee's baseline compensation.

Many people, however, fail to tap the full wealth-making potential of benefits. Some, for instance, are hidden from view because they are not categorized as benefits but are considered part of the company's employment policies. These may include parental sick leave, compassion leave, bereavement leave, Christmas gifts, and so on. Although these are not usually presented to prospective employees as benefits, you should inquire about them and compare them when considering competing job offers.

Other benefits can be extremely confusing. It is not unusual to get a fifty-page benefits booklet from your employer on medical coverage alone, for instance. Far from generating a feeling of security, this information overload creates anxiety. What's worse, benefit decisions usually have to be made at the beginning of a job, when you are more worried about where to park or about the company's dress code policies than about whether to go with an HMO or a preferred provider health plan.

Circling In on Your Benefits

Put the power of a women's circle to work, at work, by getting some of your colleagues together to review your company's benefits. A good time is during the annual open season when employees have a chance to make changes to their benefits packages. Discuss the different plans available and share the reasons for your choices of one plan over another. So often we review our benefits in isolation (if we review them at all); understanding how others are navigating the menu of options can be informative and helpful to improving our own choices.

In some cases, we may not fully appreciate the significance or value of a particular benefit. Most women think first about health insurance, for example, in view of our concern about our families and dependents. Life insurance is probably next on our list of important considerations, again because we are thinking about our children and spouses or partners. But disability insurance is often ignored, even though it is every bit as important, perhaps more so, than the first two. The risk of a woman becoming disabled is far greater than her risk of dying. First of all, you die only once, whereas you can be disabled on more than one occasion. Secondly, women are more prone to disabling conditions, such as arthritis and, yes, pregnancy, which often counts as a disability for coverage purposes. When job hunting, therefore, disability insurance is as important to look for and negotiate as health and life insurance.

This does not mean you should automatically take any benefits offered by your employer. For example, you may be adequately covered by your husband's medical plan or have no dependents, in which case life insurance may be of little value. But if you don't need a particular coverage, don't forget to negotiate for something else in its place. Opting out of medical coverage, for example, could be parlayed into several thousand dollars of additional salary at no extra cost to your employer. It never hurts to ask.

Insurance benefits you emphatically do not need, especially if they entail a cost to you, are life insurance for a dependent child or accidental death and dismemberment insurance.

Insurance benefits you emphatically do not need, especially if they entail a cost to you, are life insurance for a dependent child or accidental death and dismemberment insurance. In the first case, while the death of a child is devastating, it does not result in destitution. There is no financial loss, such as lost income, that needs to be insured. In the case of accidental death and dismemberment, the cost of insurance versus the expected benefit, should there be a claim, makes this type of insurance extremely inefficient. Any extra insurance dollars you have should be directed to simple life insurance.

Other benefits you should most definitely accept are contributions to retirement, cafeteria plans, and day care. Some day care benefits and employer contributions to a retirement plan may be free and nontaxable (be sure to check), whereas your elective contributions to retirement and cafeteria plans, also nontaxable, do reduce your take-home pay—though they are generally too beneficial to pass up. In the case of retirement plan contributions, your employer will often match what you contribute, up to a maximum. In the case of a cafeteria plan, you will be paying pretax dollars for benefits you select, such as eye care or orthodontia, that you would otherwise be purchasing after tax, which provides a saving to you.

Benefits provided by your employer that have to be paid with your after-tax dollars present a more difficult choice. Sometimes they are a good bet because your employer obtains them at a lower rate than you could as an individual. But this is not always the case. For instance, you might be able to buy life insurance over the $50,000 tax-free term amount, which many employers offer through payroll deductions. Because risks are pooled in the group, the premiums should be lower than if you bought the same coverage individually. However, adverse selection can sometimes occur in these group plans; individuals who would not qualify for coverage on their own get it through a group plan instead. This, in turn, can actually increase the cost of group coverage compared to what you can get on your own and is particularly true of the group long-term care insurance made available without underwriting to federal employees. The kinds of risk tables used to price group plans can also skew their costs. Unisex tables, for instance, will favor women when it comes to disability insurance but not when it comes to life insurance.

Therefore, do not make the automatic assumption that just because a benefit can be purchased through your employer you should accept it. Instead, get the advice of an independent insurance specialist to compare what you can purchase through your workplace and what you can obtain on your own. Very few people ask for this kind of help, but the potential savings and/or increased coverage are definitely worth it.

Investing in your human capital is an important component of your worth and your financial planning.

However you invest in your human capital—whether by paying attention to your benefits or maximizing your earnings (and ideally you will do both)—it is an important component of your worth and your financial planning. Keep your focus not just on what you have, but on what you do, and, even more important, on what you may be able to do in the future.

SUGGESTED ROUTES

www.bls.gov/oco
The *Occupational Outlook Handbook*, produced by the Bureau of Labor Statistics, provides job-specific information, including

required training and education, expected earnings, job responsibilities, and working environment. State-by-state job information is also available.

www.catalyst.org
Catalyst is an organization dedicated to expanding opportunities for women in the workplace and promoting gender equality in business.

www.makemineamillion.org
This website promotes economic independence and the success of women-owned business. Make Mine a Million $ Business is a program from Count Me In, a provider of resources, business education, and community support for women entrepreneurs.

www.payscale.com
PayScale provides statistics on average salaries by job title, experience, and location.

www.monster.com
Popular job search site that provides a benchmarking tool for comparing what you are making to the pay of others with the same job description or title.

www.womensmedia.com
WomensMedia is rich with articles, recommended books, and blogs about women in the workplace. It focuses on the issue of pay inequity and how to negotiate promotions and pay raises successfully.

Babcock, Linda, and Sara Laschever, *Women Don't Ask: Negotiation and the Gender Divide,* Princeton University Press, 2003.

Crittenden, Ann. *The Price of Motherhood: Why the Most Important Job in the World Is Still the Least Valued*, Henry Holt and Company, 2001.

Merlino, Nell. *Stepping Out of Line: Lessons for Women Who Want It Their Way in Life, in Love, and at Work*, Broadway Books, 2009.

Shipman, Claire and Katty Kay, *Womenomics: Write Your Own Rules for Success*, HarperCollins, 2009.

Chapter Five

Women Spend

Why has the female stereotype of women as black-belt spenders—one that husbands, fathers, and boyfriends love to gripe about—been perpetuated for so long? Perhaps it's because women typically do most of the shopping for the household. Or perhaps it's due to women's inherent generosity, or propensity to put others ahead of themselves. Staying within a budget requires saying "no" to children, family, and friends whom we want to please and take care of. However well-meaning or justifiable the explanation, it is nevertheless true that a good proportion of women have a spending problem.

We saw in Chapter 2 that some spending is driven by a need to secure or lock in value—"If I don't buy it now, I will never get it again (at this price, in this color, size, material, et cetera)." However, a spending problem can also exist in the absence of a fear of scarcity. Even an individual who enjoys significant wealth, who has ample income, who always has money left over at the end of the month (rather than month left over at the end of the money) still has a spending problem if she cannot account for the uses of her money. Not knowing where your money goes is as detrimental to your financial well-being as not having the money in the first place.

Knowing where your money goes and living within your means, also known as cash flow management, is one of the most important aspects of being financially savvy.

Knowing where your money goes and living within your means, also known as cash flow management, is one of the most important aspects of being financially savvy. Compound interest has been described by some as the eighth wonder of the world. But I would put living within or below your means right alongside it. Indeed, without having the money to save or invest, there is nothing on which compound interest can work its miracles. First things first.

Fortunately, expense management is also the financial strategy over which we have the most control. The ready availability of all manner of credit, combined with the pervasive culture of consumerism, makes this a much more difficult task than it used to be. But my most financially successful clients are not my richest clients; rather, they are the ones who can regulate their spending.

In this chapter, we will accord expense management the importance it deserves in your personal finances without getting into the weeds. The "101 Best Ways to Manage Your Spending" can be found in any number of resources, but not here. Where you find room in your budget is your decision. My job is to give you the tools and know-how to accomplish this task.

I must confess that I spent a good part of my career as a financial planner telling my clients, perhaps a tad smugly, "I don't do budgeting." I had this theory that creating budgets for clients to manage their expenses was like a doctor putting his patients on a diet. No amount of advice was going to make an ounce of difference if the client would not do the work herself. Furthermore,

I thought that the way a client used her money was too individual to meddle with. One person's indulgence was another's necessity.

I used to restrict my inquiry into expense management to the monthly total clients were spending on fixed, recurrent expenses. In the business world, this is called the nut: the number needed each and every month to keep the door open and the lights on. Or in this case, the nut to keep everyone housed, fed, clothed, and living productive lives. Some clients knew immediately what their nut was, some did not and had to do some calculating. Often the answer I got wouldn't make sense. The expenses were far too high for the income level, and I had to conclude they were spending too much in relation to what they earned. My cursory inquiry, in other words, was signaling a spending problem.

EXERCISE 5–1. DO YOU HAVE A SPENDING PROBLEM?

You can get a good sense of the significant money leaks in your cash management by looking at your expenditures from a bottom-up perspective, your net income from a top-down perspective, and comparing the two.

Starting with the bottom-up analysis, list the categories of goods and services that you spend your money on and how much you spend. Give the amounts in terms of monthly expenditures, even for expenses made more or less frequently (e.g., groceries, real estate taxes, car insurance premiums). Try to be as comprehensive and accurate as possible. If you do not know the amount of a given expenditure, list the category anyway and put a question mark for the amount. Do not include taxes.

Next, do a top-down analysis of your net income. This exercise requires you to get familiar with your most recent tax return. It tracks the line numbers from the 2009 Form 1040; as the form is amended, the line numbers corresponding to the income and expense categories may change. If it is not representative of your current situation—as may be the case if your income has increased or decreased significantly—try to replicate this exercise without reference to the amounts actually entered on the tax return and instead substitute estimates of the actual amounts. With your most recent federal and state tax returns in front of you, follow the instructions below:

- From "Wages, salaries, tips" on page 1, line 7, of Form 1040, list the total of your earned income. $__________

- From "Taxable interest," "Tax-exempt interest," "Ordinary dividends," "Taxable refunds, credits, or offsets," and "Alimony" on lines 8a, 8b, 9a, 10, and 11 list only those amounts you actually received and deposited in your checking account. If interest or dividends were reinvested, or you applied your state tax refund to next year's tax bill, do not include these amounts. $__________

- From "Business income," "IRA distributions," "Pension and annuities," "Rental real estate, royalties, partnerships, S corporations, trust," "Farm income," "Unemployment compensation," "Social security," and "Other income," on lines 12, 15a, 16a, 17, 18, 19, 20a, and 21, list only those amounts you actually received and deposited in your checking account. Income that was not distributed to you personally but was kept in your investment, IRA, business, trust, or real estate property account should not be counted. In the case of unemployment compensation, the 2009 tax return asks you to report the compensation in excess of $2,400. For this exercise report the full amount you received. $__________

- On "Capital gain or (loss)" and "Other gains or (losses)" on lines 13 and 14, you reported your realized gains or losses.

Do not list these numbers, but instead report any proceeds you received and deposited in your checking account from the sale of any assets. If you did not deposit the proceeds but had them reinvested, do not report them. $__________

- From all of the entries made in the "Adjusted Gross Income" section on the first page of your 1040 (i.e., the amounts entered on lines 23 to 35), take only those amounts you actually paid out of your checking or cash accounts. Most of the amounts reported in this section will not be what you paid, but will be amounts derived from other tax schedules that adjust your expenses for determining a deductible amount (e.g., moving expenses, student loan interest, tuition, and fees deduction). Determine the full amounts you paid, before any allowable deductions (e.g., your full tuition, not just the deductible amount). Amounts that represent transfers from investment accounts (such as monies from a savings or brokerage account to fund an individual retirement account (IRA) or a health savings account) or a reduction in proceeds (such as an early withdrawal penalty) should not be listed. Enter the total amount actually paid as a negative number. $__________

- From "Total tax" on page 2, line 60 of your 1040, jot down the total tax amount as a negative number. In this case, the important number is not the taxes you actually paid or had withheld, but your total tax liability for the year. $__________

- From your state tax return, find the total tax number and note it as a negative number. $__________

Add all the amounts you have listed and divide by 12. This should be a fairly accurate estimate of your monthly amount of cash available for expenses.

If your bottom-up number is greater than your top-down number, can you explain where you got money for the shortfall? Did you take money from other investment or savings accounts? Did you borrow money? Did you run up credit card balances?

Now compare the two numbers you have derived from your bottom-up and top-down analyses. How close are they? If your bottom-up number is greater than your top-down number, can you explain where you got money for the shortfall? Did you take money from other investment or savings accounts? Did you borrow money? Did you run up credit card balances?

If your bottom-up number is less than your top-down number, can you account for the discrepancy? Go back to your tax return and see if a significant amount of federal and/or state tax was overpaid. If that doesn't account for some or most of the discrepancy, did you save the difference between what you had available and what you spent? If not, your next task is to find leaks in your budget—those expenses that do not come readily to mind when you think about how you are spending your money, but nonetheless represent a significant outflow when added up.

GAIN CONTROL

Knowing where your money goes is the first step toward financial control. Any woman who has ever been a serious dieter will agree that one of the best ways to start a weight-loss program is to write down everything—absolutely everything—that she eats for the first couple of days. By seeing on paper what she eats and when (and perhaps why), she begins to see patterns that need to be changed and indulgences that need to be avoided. Even without making any appreciable alterations to her eating behavior, a woman who spends a week recording every consumed morsel often finds herself a pound or two lighter at the end of the seven days. The explanation for this is not the high caloric burn involved in the act of writing. The reason is that having to pick up a pencil or fire up the computer every time she eats makes a woman think twice about whether that dollop of dip is really worth it. Mindless eating is eliminated.

When we see what we are spending, we begin to make choices to ensure that our spending is deliberate and purposeful.

The same approach works with managing your expenses. While it may not be necessary to write down every outflow, effective cash management—like effective dieting—has two important requirements. First, our spending needs to be *visible*: it must be a highly conscious and documented act. Second, we need to make it *difficult* or, put another way, worth the effort. Mindless spending is thus eliminated. When we see what we are spending, we begin to make choices to ensure our spending is deliberate and purposeful. In terms of the paradigm we discussed in Chapter 2, we need to elevate the act of spending into the act of purchasing.

Two of the most common ways of spending—cash and credit cards—do not pass the requirements of visibility and difficulty. How often do we start the week with plenty of cash and end the week with coins at the bottom of our pocketbooks without any real sense of where the money went? Cash is also easy to spend—in fact, the demand for our cash often rises with supply. I certainly have found that when I take an extra-large amount of money from the ATM for the week, I tend to go out for lunch more often, or take taxis instead of the metro. This is arguably even more the case with credit cards, where the supply of money is usually much greater than what we have in our bank accounts. Overuse of credit cards can sometimes rise to the level of pathology, like alcoholism or sex addiction. On the other hand, one can argue that credit card spending is more visible than using cash. After all, we receive statements every month. But do we really look at them? Do we categorize each expense so it can be cross-referenced to what we have budgeted? Or do we simply glance, pay the minimum balance, and toss? In too many cases, we do the latter.

If you wish to control your money, you may wish to consider using a debit card or even old-fashioned checks in place of cash or credit cards. The disadvantage of checks is that they are a nuisance to use. They take time to write out, require proof of identity, and are sure to alienate shop clerks and other customers waiting behind you in line. On the plus side, there is no way you can be mindless or impulsive about writing a check. And having a record of the amount of your check, either in the check register or by means of carbon copies in the checkbook, also increases the visibility of check writing.

Meanwhile, debit cards, while as easy to use as credit cards, eliminate the promiscuity factor because you cannot spend more than you have in your account. (Some banks do allow you to overdraft your account with your debit card, but the expenses for the "privilege" of doing so are so ridiculously high that you are likely not to do this again.) Therefore, as with checks, you have to think before you spend. Debit card transactions also make your spending habits highly, even painfully, visible on your monthly bank statement ("I went to Starbucks three times in one day? . . . Yikes!").

Your debit card can also be tied into a budgeting software program such as Quicken or Microsoft Money. I have set up a link between my checking account and Quicken software (it's my experience that the software works better than the online version). Every time I use my debit card, the transaction is downloaded from my bank into my Quicken program. Each transaction includes the name of the vendor and the amount. I then simply categorize the transaction using the preset or self-edited budget categories in the Quicken list of expenses. If the transaction is with a vendor I have used before, I do not have to reenter the type of expense. This is far simpler than tracking credit card expenses.

Keep in mind, however, that the potential risks and costs associated with using debit cards may be greater than those of using credit cards, such as a greater liability for fraudulent use, or monthly or per-transaction fees. Go to U.S. PIRG—the federation of state public interest research groups—at www.uspirg.org for comparisons of credit and debit cards.

BENCHMARKS

Learning where you are overspending and gaining control of your expenditures is one thing, but many female clients want to know what is normal when it comes to spending. They will ask, "We're spending $10,000 a month after taxes. Is that too much?" Or, "Our housing expenses are 40 percent of our take-home pay. Is that more than other people pay?" These are, of course, questions to which there are no pat answers. They usually require a further discussion of an individual's or couple's income, stage of life, professional status, and financial goals.

Benchmarks are aspirational and normative: they set out reasonable allocations to expense categories for individuals who wish to retire comfortably and manage their debt burdens.

At the same time, the practice of benchmarking key financial statistics and ratios is a respected management tool in the business world. Comparing revenue and expense figures of a given business to averages for the appropriate industry, for instance, can help managers with their resource allocation and staffing decisions. Although individuals are not industries and do not fit so neatly into standard boxes, broad guidelines can signal to us whether our expenditures are significantly out of whack. These benchmarks are not based on what most people actually spend. Indeed, in a nation where the savings rate has been negative up until recently, few of us should wish to spend like our neighbors. Rather, the benchmarks are aspirational and normative: they set out reasonable allocations to expense categories for individuals who wish to retire comfortably and manage their debt burdens.

Here's what the experts use:

- Bankers, particularly mortgage lenders, calculate what are called front and back ratios to assess consumers' ability to take on additional debt. They recommend that to qualify for a mortgage loan, your all-in housing costs (which include your loan principal and interest, real estate taxes, and home and mortgage insurance) not exceed 28 percent of your pretax income. This is called the front ratio. The back ratio is the sum of these housing costs as well as any non-housing debt, and is not to exceed 36 percent of pretax income.

- The Credit Guy at www.creditcards.com recommends that no more than 30 percent of net income go to housing costs, with utilities to be held at 5 percent or less. He puts food at more or less the same level as transport: both should eat no more than 15 or 16 percent of your take-home pay. He leaves a large miscellaneous category of 29 percent.

- The mother-and-daughter financial team Elizabeth Warren and Amelia Warren Tyagi recommend a 50/30/20 approach in their book *All Your Worth: The Ultimate Lifetime Money Plan*. The first 50 percent is to be allocated to needs, 30 percent is allowed for wants, and the remaining 20 percent is to go to savings. The percentages are based on take-home pay.

- Charles J. Farrell, writing in the *Journal of Financial Planning* (the monthly publication of the Financial Planning Association) focuses on the savings component of budgets and recommends that between 12 and 19 percent of gross income go to savings and investment. This includes any amounts put into an employer's retirement plan, as well as the employer's match.

The above guidelines demonstrate why such benchmarks can get confusing. In some cases advice is rendered on an after-tax basis, in others it is based on pretax amounts. Some advice is quite specific (as in the guideline for expenditure on utilities), while other advice leaves a lot to interpretation—for instance, what is a want and what is a need? What constitutes savings and does it include paying off credit cards or mortgage debt? Banks emphasize benchmarks for obtaining loans, while others are interested mainly in benchmarks that apply to savings.

Based on my experience, benchmarks should be provided for all usual expenses and expressed as a percentage of after-tax income to be as comprehensive and useful as possible. I am using after-tax income because, as a well-known municipal bond management company advertises, "It's not what you make, it's what you keep" that counts. Gross income is irrelevant when it comes to making ends meet month to month.

Circling In on Budgeting

Get some friends together to share ideas on sticking to a budget. Adopt this practice from business: create what is called a common-size budget where all your expenditure categories are expressed as a percentage—not a dollar amount—of your after-tax income. This allows you to share your information with your group without feeling uncomfortable about exactly how much you are earning or spending.

However, advice based on after-tax income makes sense only if the right amount is withheld for federal and state (and in some cases local) taxes. A word, therefore, about taxes: Many employees assume that what is withheld for taxes from their paychecks is out of their control. They see it as money taken, rather than money given by their choice. They might remember that they once filled out a W-4 form claiming a certain number of withholding allowances based on their marital status and number of dependents, but the link between what they reported on their W-4 and their current paycheck is usually forgotten.

Most people don't know they can tell their payroll department what needs to be withheld from their paycheck in order to fit their tax liability.

Most people don't know they can tell their payroll department what needs to be withheld from every paycheck in order to fit their tax liability. If your payroll department is highly bureaucratic, uncreative, or unwilling to work with you, you can go to www.irs.gov and download Circular E (Publication 15-T). There you will find tables organized by the frequency of your paycheck, your filing status, and the amount of your gross income for each pay period. The appropriate table will provide the amount that should be withheld for each allowance claimed. You can pick the allowance amount closest to the sum you want withheld, and enter this number on your W-4. If necessary, you can state a certain number of allowances and also request an additional dollar amount be withheld. To get the right state withholding amount, I suggest dividing your state tax rate by your federal tax rate and multiplying the result by the amount of federal withholding per paycheck. This should give you a reasonably accurate amount of state tax to withhold every paycheck.

How do you know the proper amount that should be withheld in your case? Unfortunately, this involves work and skills (and possibly software) that you may not have. (More likely, you have the skills; it is just the work you do not want to do.) It involves doing a tax projection for each tax year, ideally a month or two before the new tax year starts, and whenever you have a significant change in your income or expense status. Doing an annual tax projection is, in my opinion, every bit as necessary to your financial confidence as preparing a budget. In fact, the second cannot be properly prepared without the first.

If you don't have the tools and/or skills to make such a projection, you can ask a tax preparer to do this for you. You may already be using a preparer to file your tax return. If, and only if, you are assured that your situation has not changed, you can look at last year's tax liability (making sure to check the amount of total taxes, not what was paid or what was owed) and use that number for this year. If you have significant investments, however, or there has been a change in tax law, this will not work.

Getting your withholding amount right (and by the way, this also applies to any estimated tax payments you make) makes understanding what you are spending and what you can spend that much easier. When your taxes get out of sync with your cash flow—you are paying too much this year and are getting a refund next year, or you are paying too little today and have to cough up extra tomorrow—it becomes difficult, if not impossible, to keep within a budget. And once budgeting gets difficult, people often abandon it altogether.

Now that we have established how to ensure that your take-home pay is the appropriate amount available for your budget decisions, let's look at some benchmark ranges for the most common expense categories (see Table 5.1). These are consensus guidelines based on a compilation of what many financial advisors recommend. They are not averages of what people are actually spending.

GETTING EVEN MORE SPECIFIC

We have talked a lot about the importance of knowing what you are spending. It's now time to go beyond having a pretty good idea of your expenses. Start with that all-purpose expense category—the one where so many of our sins seem to disappear—namely, cash. One of my clients calls this category her "walking around money," but given its size relative to her other uses of funds, it appears she is doing a lot of walking.

Table 5.1. Benchmark Ranges for Expenses by Category

Expense	Range, as Percentage of Take-Home Income	Comments
Housing	25–30 percent	Includes taxes, insurance, utilities. Most people start out at the higher percentage when first owning or renting, but the percentage should go down over time.
Savings	10–20 percent	If you have credit card debt, any payments toward the principal should go here and should be made before other savings. Do not include retirement plan contributions that are tax-deferred, nor employer contributions or your match. The later you start saving, the closer this number should be to the higher end of the range.
Living expenses	30–40 percent	Includes food, clothing, transportation, out-of-pocket medical, and education expenses.
Emergency/insurance	10–20 percent	Includes insurance premiums and unanticipated, but needed, expenses, such as repairs. This is not your emergency fund, which should be funded up front and not as an ongoing expense.
Pleasure/personal	5–10 percent	Includes vacation, entertainment.

EXERCISE 5–2. WHERE IS YOUR CASH GOING?

Answer the following:

- How much cash would you estimate you spend in a given week?
- Looking at your last two or three bank statements, what was the total amount typically withdrawn over this period?
- Did you write any checks made out to cash? If you are in the habit of taking cash back from checks you deposit, try to remember what amount of cash that was. (This may be hard, as you may only see a net deposit on your bank account. This habit is important to break in the interest of greater visibility of your use of money.)
- List in dollars, and not as a percentage, what those cash withdrawals were spent on. Are you able to account for all the cash withdrawn?
- As a percentage, what was the amount of cash withdrawn in relation to monthly take-home income?

Having accounted for your use of cash, add this information to your other documented expenditures to come up with a complete use-of-funds statement for at least a calendar quarter. This means going through your checkbook and/or bank statement and your credit card statements and categorizing all your expenditures. Break them down into the benchmark categories listed in Table 5.1.

Compare the actual uses of your money, as a percentage of your take-home pay, to the benchmarks cited above. Are there any major discrepancies between actual and benchmarks? What do you need to do to bring your expenses into the ranges suggested above?

The medical profession advises us that we need to know our "numbers": our body mass index, blood pressure, and good and bad cholesterol levels. The same numerical awareness is needed for our financial health.

The medical profession advises us that we need to know our "numbers": our body mass index, blood pressure, and good and bad cholesterol levels. The same numerical awareness is needed for our financial health. You should know the following, readily and fairly accurately, without going back to records:

- How much money you are taking home (e.g., wages or other sources of income that you run through your bank account or otherwise spend)
- Your monthly living expenses
- Your monthly fixed expenses: mortgage, property taxes, car loan, student loan, et cetera
- The amount and timing of your lump-sum fixed expenses (e.g., annual insurance premiums)
- How much cash you spend per month
- What that cash is being used for
- Your tax liability for the current year (not what you paid last year, but what you will owe this year)

VALUES REVISITED

Most of us feel constrained by our expenses: there just doesn't seem to be much wiggle room in how we spend our money. If we think in less dualistic terms, however—no longer dividing expenses into variable and fixed, or discretionary and non-discretionary—we may find more elasticity in how we are able to use money than we thought possible. Consider that there may in fact be three categories of spending rather than just two. The first includes the necessary expenses for which amounts are fixed—mortgages, insurance premiums, and so on. Next are the expenses over which we have total control, both in terms of deciding to incur the expense and the amount spent. A third category can occupy the space between the two: necessary expenses, the amount of which is up to us. A significant portion of our monthly budget falls into this category: money spent on food, clothing, and transportation, to name just a few. We can't live without these things, but how much we spend is largely in our control.

I would go further still. There is a large discretionary component in just about every category of expenses. Even when it comes to fixed obligations, such as mortgage or car loan payments, there is always the option to pay them off or refinance.

Having evaluated the spending patterns and habits of hundreds of individuals and couples, I assure you that people's budgets are as individual and distinct as their thumbprints. I have come to see people's spending as a unique form of self-expression. Whether it expresses what they value and admire, or fear, or dislike, is another matter.

EXERCISE 5–3. WHAT ARE YOUR MONTHLY EXPENSES REALLY FOR?

Go back to the list you made in Exercise 5–1 of all your expenses by category, amount spent monthly, and percentage of total

Table 5.2. One Woman's Monthly Expenses, Using Quicken Software

Expense Category	Monthly Amount	Percentage	Why Spent?
Food	$ 400	7.6	
Utilities	$ 882	16.7	
Housing costs	$ 960	18.1	
Home improvement	$1,010	19.1	
Auto	$1,088	20.6	
Insurance	$ 142	2.7	
Clothing	0	0	
Charity	0	0	
Entertainment	$ 20	0.4	
Eating out	$ 157	3.0	
Gifts	$ 150	2.8	
Medical	$ 145	2.7	
Personal	$ 137	2.6	
Pet care	$ 200	3.8	
TOTAL	$5,291	100	

monthly expenditure. Add an extra column to the right and label it "Why Spent?"

Table 5.2 is an actual table of one woman's monthly expenses as recorded in Quicken. (Note that there is no category for cash, since she has taken the recommended step of using a debit card for all her cash purchases so she could download her transactions by vendor from her bank account.)

Referring back to the values we discussed in Chapter 3, can any of these expenses be associated with those values? Can what we value be used to fill in the "Why Spent?" column? Here's how the woman on the Quicken budget completed the fourth column:

Table 5.3. One Woman's Monthly Expenses, Using Quicken Software – With Justifications

Expense Category	Monthly Amount	Percentage	Why Spent?
Food	$ 400	7.6	Have to
Utilities	$ 882	16.7	Have to
Housing costs	$ 960	18.1	Independence
Home improvement	$1,010	19.1	Creativity
Auto	$1,088	20.6	Have to
Insurance	$ 142	2.7	Have to
Clothing	0	0	
Charity	0	0	

Table 5.3. ***(continued)***

Expense Category	Monthly Amount	Percentage	Why Spent?
Entertainment	$ 20	0.4	Not sure
Eating out	$ 157	3.0	Not sure
Gifts	$ 150	2.8	Family
Medical	$ 145	2.7	Health
Personal	$ 137	2.6	Growth (self)
Pet care	$ 200	3.8	Family
TOTAL	$5,291		

We don't just earn or use money to pay bills; we use it to make choices about what we value.

Clearly, associating what you spend your money on with what you value does not result in a neatly wrapped and bow-tied paradigm. Some expenses can be dropped readily into a value category—for instance, considering medical expenses as supporting your value for health, or insurance costs as important for security—but others take some stretching. Looking at housing costs as a means of achieving or maintaining your independence is certainly not a usual or automatic way of thinking about our uses of money. But in trying to make these expense/value associations, we gain a sense of money as having the potential for purpose and direction in our lives. We don't just earn or use money to pay bills; we use it to make choices about what we value.

There is one category of expense, however, that you should readily associate with what you value: this is the money you "spend" on savings. You may think of savings as having a more concrete, specific purpose: saving for retirement, for example, or saving for a second home. But underneath the *what* is the *why*: why do we want to have money for retirement? Why do we want a second home? What aspect of ourselves and our strongest beliefs about a worthwhile life can be expressed in the way we will someday use our savings?

Like the woman in our example, you may find yourself filling in the "Why Spent?" column with several "Have to's" or "Not sure's." These answers may indicate that you feel you don't have a choice or that you don't have a good reason for the money spent. Or they may alert you to expenses you don't feel good about, which means they are worth examining further. You may ask, for instance: How constrained am I when it comes to these expenditures? Is there room for elevating some of them from a necessity to a higher level of purpose? The answer for just about anyone is certainly "yes." It is not an easy exercise, but certainly one worth doing.

The other purpose of this exercise is to compare the way you spend your money to the way you would spend your time. In Chapter 3 you created a pie of values, having established allocations or priorities for these values based on the way you would spend a free day. If you were to create a pie chart of your expenditures, as categorized by the values they represent, how similar would the two pies be? Is what you are spending money on congruent with your values, or do the two pies tell different stories? What are some ways you might redirect your uses of money to be more consistent with what you value? What can you do immediately, and what can be done over time?

By seeing your spending as a way of realizing and expressing values, you put yourself in charge of your budget rather than the other way around.

Decision Point ***When does it make sense for me to borrow money?***

There is, perhaps, no single issue that thwarts people's path to financial success more than the borrowing of money. Whereas taking on debt used to be a rare and solemn event, today almost all of us have debt of some form or another. Most of us don't even think twice about it anymore. The crucial question becomes: When is debt, as Martha Stewart might say, a good thing?

We are continually told about the wonders of leverage, how by putting a little of our own money into certain assets and using other people's money to finance the rest, we can significantly increase the rate of return on our investments. Another persistent notion is that borrowing money is a good idea when it is tax-deductible. "I need a mortgage," my clients solemnly assure me, "because I pay too much in taxes." Young adults are also told that getting a credit card is a financial rite necessary to obtain a good credit rating, which is in turn necessary if they want to borrow more money down the road.

But we have become a nation of overextended debtors, with the savings rate in this country having gone into negative territory over the past few years. (A negative savings rate implies that we are living beyond our means, which in turn implies that we are borrowing to cover our expenses.) The significant market downturn in 2008 started because millions of American homeowners could no longer afford the mortgages on their homes—something we grew up believing was a necessary and responsible part of being a financially mature adult.

So, when is borrowing money good, when is it okay, and when is it just plain bad?

First, should you ever borrow money if you have the money to pay for the thing you want? To answer this question you have to compare the after-tax return you expect to make on your own money with the after-tax cost of using other people's money. Generally speaking, the interest on mortgages, home-equity lines, business loans, and, in some cases, education loans is tax-deductible, whereas interest on personal loans, car loans, and credit cards is not. If the interest is tax-deductible, multiply the loan rate by 1-minus-your-marginal-tax-rate to calculate your after-tax loan cost. (For example, if your marginal tax rate is 25 percent, and the interest rate on your mortgage loan is 8 percent, your after-tax loan cost is 6 percent, or 75 percent of 8 percent.) Compare this number to what you are making with your investments or savings. Express the latter number as a percentage and multiply it by 1-minus-your-tax-rate, unless your cash or investment is tax exempt, in which case no adjustment for taxes is necessary.

Generally, if your borrowing cost exceeds the return on your funds, it does not make sense to borrow. Use your own money. However—and this is an important caveat—there can be good reasons to keep your cash available, namely emergencies and liquidity, even if it is returning less than your loan cost. For this reason, financial planners—myself included—often advise that your borrowing cost needs to be at least 1 to 2 percent higher than your investment returns before you use your own funds.

The analysis can get tricky if you are comparing variable investment returns to fixed borrowing costs, fixed investment returns to variable borrowing costs, or variable returns to variable costs, since you cannot know beforehand what the spread between your cost and your return will be for the life of the loan. But if your loan costs can go up, compare the possible higher costs of the loan with what you expect to earn on your money (remembering that when loan costs go up, often the expected return on your investments goes down).

The comparison between using your own money and borrowed money becomes moot when you do not have any money in the first place. In these cases, borrowing makes sense if the assets acquired are expected to appreciate, especially if at a rate greater than your borrowing costs. Houses generally fall into this category (although there has been some doubt about this, of late). Loans for college education or professional training are also good bets, if you assume that the investment in a degree or new skills will result in increased earning potential over a significant period of time. Borrowing for a sound business venture or to make a long-term investment can also pass the test, as long as you've taken care to ascertain that you really can expect an appreciation on the financed assets.

CAN YOU RELATE?

In the 1990s, the credit card industry launched an aggressive effort to reach lower-income users who needed credit but who would be likely to carry a monthly balance, thus generating higher revenues in interest and fees. One of the primary target markets was single women.—For a New Thrift, Confronting the Debt Culture, Institute for American Values, 2008.

But what about cars, and other large purchases, that depreciate or are consumed? First, consider whether you really need the item, or need one as expensive as the one you're looking at. Second, compare the time over which you will enjoy its benefits with the time over which you must pay the loan. If the loan is likely to last longer than the benefits, it is probably not a good idea to borrow. Take an extreme example: in the case of a night out or a restaurant meal, the enjoyment lasts only as long as the evening or the meal (unless, of course, it is the night you are proposed to!). But if you add the cost to a credit card balance, you could be paying it off over months to come. If you will still be paying for anything long after you have swallowed it, worn it, or traveled in or to it, don't borrow for it.

A mother knows that it does not make good parenting sense to punish a child three weeks after an infraction, or to give him a treat a month before or after good behavior. Likewise, it does not make good financial sense to separate the benefit of a purchase and payment for that purchase. The gap in either case leads to discouragement and frustration. It also leads to a continuation of bad behavior. So the next time you see a furniture or appliance store ad that shouts, "Nothing down and no interest for two years!" and you decide that this is a great financing deal because it's "free," think again. The numbers may make a kind of sense, but how will you feel about that sofa two years and many spills later when you have to begin paying for it? My bet is that you'll feel like you are buying a secondhand sofa at a new sofa price.

Decision Point *Should I do my taxes myself?*

There is one in every crowd. Believe it or not, for every seventy Americans who hate or dislike preparing their income taxes, there's one who reports "loving it." (I think I may have once dated that person. As I remember, he also had a pet boa constrictor and worked for the Department of Motor Vehicles.)

While few of us *love* doing taxes, it remains legitimate to ask whether we *should* prepare our own taxes each year. But before we discuss this question, let's get one thing straight. When I refer to "doing your own taxes," I am not referring to sitting down with pencil and paper. Don't even consider filing the old-fashioned way unless you file the very simplest tax return (such as the 1040EZ or 1040A). By "doing your own taxes," I mean using an IRS-approved commercial software program and/or the IRS e-filing program.

CAN YOU RELATE?

Spending money is at times an activity unto itself with no or very little connection to buying anything in particular. Kids, especially, are apt to view it this way. My daughter would get $25 from her grandmother and then figure out how to spend it, searching for items that cost exactly $25 with little or no real regard to what she in fact wanted. Gift cards have capitalized on this tendency to spend for spending's sake: they do not even give kids a chance to think about other uses for a gift of what is essentially money. Worse still, they have to spend exactly the amount of the gift card. Any more or less is gravy to the retailer.

An IRS-approved software program is necessary to avoid the most basic mathematical and omission mistakes usually made by pencil-and-paper filers. Such a program will also tell you if you are subject to the alternative minimum tax (AMT), which you would have no way of knowing by filling in a paper 1040 form. Tax preparation software also has simple diagnostic tools to alert you to possible deductions or credits that you missed or red flags that may catch the attention of the IRS.

CAN YOU RELATE?

My niece was obsessed with all things technological and cutting-edge: camera phones, iPods, TiVo. Every time a new electronic gadget came out, she would begin her passionate appeals to her mother by explaining why she absolutely needed it. Immediately! She liked to argue that buying the item would actually save money. "Mom, if we buy it today, we will save $200! Mom, there's a 50 percent saving! Mom, we can get it at Best Buy for 20 percent off!"

One day my sister hit upon a successful defense. To one of her daughter's pleas she replied: "Show me the savings! I want to see the money you save so that I can put it right into your college fund." My niece did not ask again.

But should you use this software to do your taxes yourself, or should you simply go to H&R Block or another tax preparer and spend your valuable time doing something more enjoyable?

One of my clients clearly falls into the latter camp. "When it comes to taxes," she says, "I don't know what I don't know. Actually, it's even worse than that. I don't have any freaking idea." This may be a wise observation about her limitations. But is she being smart in her approach?

CAN YOU RELATE?

Fifty or more years ago it was a rite of passage for people nearing retirement to hold mortgage-burning parties to celebrate the last payment made on their mortgage. Today it is a hotly debated question whether it makes sense ever to pay off a mortgage. It is said to require a careful analysis of tax impacts, the rate of return earned by your investments compared to the rate on your mortgage, and your need for liquidity.

What isn't usually factored into the analysis is the immeasurable benefit of being debt-free if or when your circumstances change for the worse. The ability to dial down your spending in the face of poor investment returns or an unforeseen emergency may be worth considerably more over time to your financial success, not to mention your peace of mind, than the above-average returns you project for your investments.

If she were to do her own taxes, she might learn about the way deductions and credits work to limit her tax liability. She might learn about the best allocation of her expenses between her own return and that of her business. She might also learn about the costs of being under-withheld or failing to make adequate estimated payments. The beauty of modern software is that it contains a plethora of help features and links that explain many of the things you need to know in plain language, making the whole process more like a tutorial. As a result, you will be amazed at what you can learn, both about tax and about your personal finances.

At the very least, or as a start, I recommend you enter the data on your W-2 form (the tax report provided by your employer in late January) and your 1099 forms (the reports provided by your bank, credit union, and brokers) into the tax software or worksheets provided by your tax preparer. By finding and entering the appropriate data, you gain a real appreciation for what you are being paid, what is being withheld, and what your investments and savings are doing. If you simply hand these forms to your tax preparer, you give up a good opportunity for financial self-assessment.

If you do decide to use a tax preparer, however, it is important that you at least understand the two functions of tax professionals. One is *tax compliance*, which is the process of making sure your income and expense information is reported accurately and on time to the IRS. The other is *tax planning*, which involves developing strategies to legally minimize your tax liability. The first is done by looking backward: the preparer uses last year's information to prepare this April's tax return. The second is done by looking forward: the preparer projects your liability for next year or the years following based on what you do this year. This second function takes a higher level of thinking and creativity than the first, and is arguably more important.

If you go to a tax preparer, make sure that she or he performs both the compliance and planning functions. Ask your preparer to project what you will owe at the end of the year and not just give you the figure for what you owe for last year. Make sure that the projection is not just a simple safe-harbor number based on last year's tax return. (By "safe-harbor," I mean the number that will eliminate any penalty for underpayment but will not necessarily eliminate a large over- or underpayment of taxes owed.) Make sure to tell the preparer not just what happened last year, but what you expect to do this year. Then, together with the preparer's help, adjust the withholdings from your pay and/or your estimated tax payments so that by year-end (or January 15 in the case of estimates) you have paid the IRS, and the state, if applicable, more or less what you owe for the year.

Getting a big tax refund might seem like cause for celebration, but is in fact a sign of poor money management, as is having to pay a big sum with your return. If you pay too much or too little in taxes, you will find that your annual budget discipline disappears. Either you have last year's money available for this year's expenses, or this year's money is needed for last year's expenses. It therefore becomes impossible to know whether or not you are on track with your cash flow management.

In the following instances, hiring a tax professional almost always makes sense because of the complexity of the tax forms and the opportunity for some beneficial tax planning:

- You are self-employed and/or work from home.

- You have investments or accounts that require reporting on forms other than Schedule B (i.e., limited partnership interests, trust accounts).

- You have children between eighteen and twenty-four who work and/or go to college and/or have investment income.

- You are between the ages of 59½ and 70½ (the sweet spot of retirement when IRS rules about taking too little or too much, too early or too late, from your retirement accounts are suspended). It is possible to do some creative income and expense planning to minimize your taxes. Make sure, as stated above, that your tax professional is not just a compliance guy or gal, but will do some planning and projecting as well.

SUGGESTED ROUTES

www.annualcreditreport.com
Established by the three major credit agencies, AnnualCreditReport.com is the one and only official site for obtaining a credit report. By law, you are entitled to one free credit report a year from each of the three nationwide reporting agencies: Equifax, TransUnion, and Experian. Do not be distracted by other offers for "free" reports: often a first report is free, but monthly charges will ensue for the dubious benefit of having your credit regularly monitored.

www.irs.gov
The IRS website is much friendlier and more informative than you might think. Among other services, it provides tax forms and detailed instructions.

www.nfcc.org
The National Foundation for Credit Counseling website is the place to visit first if you have a debt or credit card problem, before going to any commercial credit counselor or consolidator.

www.quicken.intuit.com
Intuit is the manufacturer of the popular budgeting tool Quicken, which is available either as a free online tool or as software you can purchase. Click on "Compare Products" to determine which product is best suited to your budgeting needs.

Blayney, Eleanor. *Home Budget Workbook: A Straightforward Guide to Create and Maintain a Practical Budget*, Peter Pauper Press, 2010.

Mellan, Olivia, and Sherry Christie. *Overcoming Overspending: A Winning Plan for Spenders and Their Partners*, Walker & Company, 1995.

Chapter Six

Women Invest

Rational spending may be the way to hold on to your money, but investing is an effective way to grow your nest egg.

Investment returns are gender-neutral. It doesn't matter whether the dollars invested come from a seventy-year-old grandmother on a fixed income or a twenty-year-old college boy via his e-trading account. Seminars, books, or websites with titles like "Investing for Women" should, therefore, be regarded with suspicion. In fact, what often makes these offerings "for women" is that they are basic or introductory. They should simply be called "Basic Investing" so women—or men—can decide whether the information they contain is appropriate for them.

GENDER DIFFERENCES IN INVESTING

The sexism inherent in the titles of such programs does hint at a real difference between men and women in relation to investing: women are less confident and comfortable with the subject. A 2005 study of gender and investing by Merrill Lynch surveyed women and men with either sole or joint responsibility for investment decisions and annual incomes of at least $75,000. A slight minority of men but a significant majority of women said they wanted to spend as little time as possible managing their investments.

Many women tell me: "I need someone to invest my money for me. That stuff is just way too complicated, and I simply don't have the time." Rarely, if ever, have I heard the same complaint from a male client. Men appear to approach investing with much less trepidation and much more ease. In fact, they often find investing fun.

"Women look at money as a lake, perceiving it as a finite resource. Men look at it as a river, constantly renewing." —Liz Perle

---

Why this gender difference exists is not entirely clear. One explanation for women's lack of confidence might be a pervasive cultural norm, largely unquestioned before the 1970s, that only men invest. Or perhaps women are reluctant to invest because they have a different perception of money. In her book *Money, A Memoir: Women, Emotions, and Cash*, Liz Perle states: "Women look at money as a lake, perceiving it as a finite resource. Men look at it as a river, constantly renewing." It makes sense that if women are preoccupied with conserving money, they will be reluctant to risk loss to grow it. A man, on the other hand, who regards money as a renewable resource will not share this reluctance.

There is a surprising twist to this story. The same Merrill Lynch study that highlighted women's distaste for investing also found that women who do invest are *better at it than men*! The study noted that, compared to men:

- Women investors make fewer mistakes.
- Women sell their losing investments sooner.
- Women are more cautious about concentrated holdings.

- Women are less likely to buy a hot stock without doing research first.
- Women trade less.

Furthermore, the study showed that once women make mistakes—selling too late or making an impulsive investment—they are far less likely to repeat them. (As an aside, one wonders if the female advantage was not underestimated in the study based on men's greater reluctance to admit mistakes.)

Brad M. Barber at University of California, Davis, and Terrance Odean at University of California, Berkeley, in a 2001 paper in the *Quarterly Journal of Economics* titled "Boys Will Be Boys: Gender, Overconfidence, and Common Stock Investment," documented that men's investment activity was almost 150 percent greater than women's. This overactivity costs money. As a result, women's portfolios returned 1.4 percent more than men's portfolios. Single women did even better, with 2.3 percent greater gains.

There are two practical lessons for single men in this research: either get married or behave more like a woman. Apparently, one of the world's richest men, Warren Buffett, has already figured this out. A forthcoming book on the success of the Oracle of Omaha is slated to be titled *Warren Buffett Invests Like a Girl.*

Investing can be done slowly, quietly, and sensibly—with no loftier goal than to achieve average results—yet still allow one to achieve financial goals.

Perhaps women will be less spooked by investing if they learn that it doesn't have to be a competitive, aggressive game played to beat the street, nor does it involve swimming with the sharks. Money does not have to be "mad" or "fast." Our role model for being smart does not have to be a Jim Cramer, who every night appears on the TV show *Mad Money*, his shirt sleeves rolled up, screaming about stocks as if they were scrapping players in a hockey game. Investing can be done slowly, quietly, and sensibly—with no loftier goal than to achieve average results—yet still allow one to achieve financial goals.

While this chapter focuses on helping you become more confident when it comes to investing, I'm not recommending you always do the investing yourself. Again, the role of a trusted CFP® professional can be invaluable in helping you construct a portfolio that answers to your needs, values, and ability to bear losses. Furthermore, a professional advisor will have the necessary dispassion that you do not when it comes to managing your money. An advisor, however, cannot—and should not—do it all for you. You must be prepared, armed with the fundamental principles of investing and a knowledge of the markets, to manage your manager.

YOUR INVESTMENT KNOWLEDGE

To many women, investing seems arcane, impossibly technical, and replete with numbers. It is not coincidental, in my view, that the format of most investment TV shows is very similar to sports coverage: there are the same intense talking heads with a busy backdrop of charts and graphs and an endless flow of streaming statistics at the bottom of the screen. These shows speak primarily to men, leaving women uncertain as to how to participate in the investment world.

Try the following exercise to assess what you may or may not know about investing, but perhaps think you should.

EXERCISE 6–1. WHAT DO YOU NEED TO UNDERSTAND?

Consider the following list of investment terms and concepts. Put a check mark in the first column for terms you are familiar with and understand. Put a check mark in the second column for terms you think you need to understand in order to be a confident, capable investor.

Investment Concept	Understand?	Need to Understand?
P/E ratios		
Growth		
Value		
Small cap		
Micro cap		
Large cap		
Emerging markets		
Alpha		
Beta		
Earnings momentum		
Dividend yield		
10-K statement		

Investment Concept	**Understand?**	**Need to Understand?**
90-day moving average		
Market capitalization		
Debt-to-equity ratio		
Bond duration		
Interest rate risk		
Equity premium		
Default risk		
EBITDA		
Limit order		
Stop loss order		
Market order		
Selling short		
Puts		
Calls		
Future contracts		

For Extra Credit:

Dead cat bounce		
Falling knife		
Sucker's rally		
Buy on news, sell on rumor		

Add up the number of check marks in each column and subtract the number in the first column from the second.

If you are like most women, your score will be positive, perhaps significantly so. What you understand about investing is overwhelmed by what you think you need to understand. This confidence gap has probably kept you from making investment decisions or has kept you from investing altogether.

A score of zero, or very close to zero, might be achieved by two very different types of women. The first may know a lot about investing, and values what she knows. The second knows very little, but does not care about she doesn't know. Ironically, neither is likely to suffer a confidence gap when it comes to investing.

I rarely see a negative score. If this is your case, you are a woman who may know a lot but does not think she knows the right things. The truth is, you probably know all you need to know . . . and maybe even more.

Circling In on Investing

Joining or creating an investment club can be a great way to learn more about markets and securities and to practice for the real thing: managing your own investment or retirement accounts. You are not likely to make a fortune in such a club, and there may be a lot more talk than actual investing going on. But it is a great way to blend two activities that often stand far apart in most women's minds: having fun and investing.

BASIC INVESTMENT CONCEPTS YOU CAN UNDERSTAND AND NEED TO UNDERSTAND

Putting technical terms aside for a moment, there are two seemingly contradictory theories that, when understood, will go a long way toward helping you navigate the world of investing. The time you take to understand these concepts will more than pay off in saved time when it comes to building and maintaining your investment portfolio. They are:

The market for investing is efficient.

The market for investing is inefficient.

Although these statements are seemingly contradictory, both need to be factored into the way you manage your investments.

Market efficiency is the premise that it is impossible for individual investors to outperform the market consistently.

Let's begin with a discussion of the first concept: market efficiency. I spent the entire two years of my MBA program mastering the theoretical and empirical justifications for this hypothesis, but the idea can be stated in simple terms. Market efficiency is the premise that it is impossible for individual investors to outperform the market consistently. A financial market, by the way, is simply a venue in which financial assets, such as stocks, bonds, options, commodities, and so on, are traded. Examples include the New York Stock Exchange or the U.S. government bond market.

Competition in financial markets for returns is vast and fierce. Millions of analysts and traders are constantly evaluating information about companies and sectors in order to be the first to know and thereby profit from their knowledge. According to the efficient market hypothesis, however, information is so abundant and instantaneous that it is impossible for investors to purchase undervalued securities or sell them at inflated prices. Thus, it is impossible to outperform the overall market through security picking or market timing. Everyone will arrive at the finish line at more or less the same time.

The efficient market hypothesis that no one can consistently beat the market seems to be contradicted, however, by the obvious fact that scores of people wake up every day believing and behaving as though they can. Why do stock analysts do research? Why does your broker tell you he has a great tip? Why does your husband even listen to him? The reason is that they believe that the market is inefficient—that market forces sometimes drive asset prices above or below their true market value, allowing one person to make more money than the next guy.

The discipline known as behavioral finance points out that market inefficiency is more often a product of investors behaving irrationally, that trends that contradict the efficient market hypothesis are often due to emotion—overconfidence in male investors, for instance, or the propensity of investors to exaggerate certain risks and ignore others, or fear. The common behavioral tics of investors make for lively and interesting speeches at financial conferences and get a lot of laughs, but the thought that markets are irrational can be depressing and leaves us wondering whether we should get involved at all.

Markets are inefficient in the short term, but over time they revert to efficiency.

After twenty-five years of studying and advising on markets and investments, however, I am convinced there is truth in both these seemingly opposite theories: markets can be both efficient and inefficient. The pattern most often seen is that markets are inefficient in the short term, but over time they revert to efficiency. Put another way, markets often initially overreact, both on the upside and the downside, due to investors' greed or fear. It is easy for investors to get caught up in the mood of a market and buy or sell without regard to the underlying value of the securities simply because others are doing so. Yet over the long term, market rationality is restored and stock prices once again become accurate reflections of the true underlying value of securities. This time period is usually a matter of years, not months or quarters. Some advisors and economists consider a five-year period long enough for market rationality and efficiency to prevail; others are more cautious and think in terms of ten years. The latter is important, because if we are to rely on market efficiency in our investing, we have to be prepared to wait through the appropriate time period to let it happen.

The realization that markets are efficient keeps us realistic and grounded: trying to beat the market is a loser's game. Our loss is not just in sub-market returns, but also in what we spend in time and money on products, strategies, and advice that has us thinking we can do significantly better than someone else. Getting the average market return is the best we can do over the long term (and surprisingly, according to one study, a significantly better result than that achieved by most investors). The realization that human emotion often leads to market inefficiency alerts us to our own subjective foibles as investors, and to the fact that market trends are at times the product of the irrational forces of greed and fear. The severe market downturn of 2008 may be a case in point.

Accepting that markets are efficient over the long term and that it is next to impossible for the average investor to do any better than the markets, how should we invest? In the 1950s and 1960s, an economist named Harry Markowitz introduced a theory of financial markets and a way to construct optimal portfolios known as modern portfolio theory. What Markowitz and his followers showed was that risk for individual stock returns has two components: systematic risk that affects all stocks, such as interest rates, recessions, or wars, and unsystematic risks or risks specific to individual stocks, such as the risk that Steve Jobs dies in a plane crash or that a popular drug is implicated in the death of children. Markowitz went on to show that the effect of these specific risks can be minimized through stock diversification or by investing in various industries, countries, and so on.

Combining the knowledge that markets are efficient in the long term and that diversification minimizes risk, the logical conclusion is that when we invest we should invest in as many assets within a particular market as possible. This is also known as holding the market. This third proposition, for all its apparent simplicity, is actually a highly sophisticated concept that has been studied, challenged, discarded, and resurrected many times over the past seventy years. But it is an eminently sensible and efficient way to approach investing.

WHICH MARKETS DO WE INVEST IN?

Using the broad principles learned above, how do we now actually go about investing? Which markets do we invest in and in what quantities?

There are three types of markets in which we can invest: cash, bonds, and stocks. Some financial analysts would argue that real estate and commodities should be added to represent the full spectrum of economic possibilities. In my experience, however, individual investors are well advised to build their portfolios with just the basic three, leaving the two other categories to more sophisticated institutional investors.

Even within these three categories, tremendous differentiation and complexity exists because of the growth of financial innovation, the speed of information, the creation and proliferation of organized exchanges, and the globalization of trade and economic activity. But let's stick to basics.

Cash can include a variety of short-term obligations, from Treasury bills, to bank notes, to money market funds, to foreign currency. The one common denominator for these instruments is that they have a maturity or market life of one year or less. Because of this extremely short maturity, the values of these instruments stay very stable. Each unit of investment in a money market, for example, is always held at a constant $1 par value.

Bonds, on the other hand, have maturities of a year or more. Issuers of bonds are the federal government and its agencies, municipalities, and corporations, all of which issue bonds in exchange for investment capital. Bonds can also be grouped according to the country of issuance; domestic bonds consist of all U.S. fixed-income obligations, and foreign bonds are those that originate anywhere else in the world.

When it comes to stock or equity, for many years the only market to consider was the U.S. stock market. With the growth of global economic activity, however, stock markets have been created in many countries outside the U.S. Many financial analysts invest in international stocks in both developed countries (e.g., Western European countries, Canada, Japan, Australia) and emerging economies (e.g., Eastern European countries, China, Mexico, India, Pakistan, Brazil, the Middle East, and Africa).

Aside from the domestic and foreign stock distinction, stocks can also be divided into large caps (stocks of large companies) and small caps (stocks of small companies). Stocks can also be categorized as either growth or value, depending on the industry and management characteristics of the company issuing the stock. For example, the stock of a rapidly growing company that does not pay dividends but plows its earnings back into the company is usually characterized as a growth stock. On the other hand, equity issued by a slower-growth, stable company, in which earnings are distributed to stockholders through dividends, is more likely to be seen as a value stock. Another definition of a value stock refers to the equity of a company that is considered to be an opportunistic buy, because of unique circumstances, such as new legislation or a change in patent. But this brief primer on different types of stocks is for your information only; you do not need to get overly preoccupied with this distinction when it comes to smart investing.

Choosing which markets to invest in and in what proportion—an activity called asset allocation—is one of the most important decisions an investor can make.

Choosing which markets to invest in and in what proportion—an activity called asset allocation—is one of the most important decisions an investor can make. It is also often the most confusing. How many equity classes are too many? How many bond classes are too few? Your answer to these questions depends in part on the size of your investable portfolio: the more you have to invest, the more differentiation you can accommodate in the portfolio. But the more important criterion for adding asset classes to your portfolio is true value added. If by adding a market or class of security to your portfolio you can increase your expected return or lower the risk of your investments or both, then the addition makes sense: it has improved your expected outcome. If, on the other hand, the only reason you add a class of asset is simply because it has been defined as different and distinct from your other investments—by product providers or salespeople or the latest investment newsletter—you are merely incurring more cost and confusion in your portfolio management.

As in so many other aspects of personal financial management, keeping it simple does not mean being simpleminded. You can keep it simple by investing in the following four markets: money markets, U.S. government bonds, U.S. stocks, and international stocks. Each of these categories represents a huge market, but they are sufficiently different in their return and risk characteristics to be considered positive additions to your portfolio. Furthermore, these markets are efficient in the sense discussed above: they are broadly and continuously traded and, therefore, reflective of reliable value over the long term. Using this efficient market criterion generally eliminates from consideration emerging market securities, micro-stocks or stocks of extremely small companies, private equity or debt, and even individual municipal securities. Information is not widely disseminated and trading is sporadic with respect to these investments, leading to erratic and unpredictable returns. In our simple, but not simpleminded, approach, unpredictable implies unacceptable risk.

To determine in what proportions to invest in these four categories, start by dividing your portfolio into two parts. The first will consist of money you will need to spend or withdraw from the portfolio within the next five to ten years. You may require this money for tuition payments or a down payment on a home, for example. If you are retired, you might need living expenses not covered by your pension or social security benefits. (Exclude any money you need more or less immediately or any set aside for an emergency fund; these sums are not part of your investable portfolio and belong strictly in a separate bank account or money market account.) The second part of your portfolio will consist of investments that are truly long-term and not needed for the foreseeable future.

Invest the first part of your portfolio in money markets and U.S. government bonds, since these investments are safer than stocks and more likely to hold their value over the short term. Put the amounts you need in the next year in money markets so that these are readily available. Put the rest into U.S. government bonds. You might consider using municipal bonds, which are not federally taxable, but it is hard to get the proper amount of diversification with individual municipal bonds, and the markets for these bonds are often inefficient because they are not centralized and are highly fragmented.

Part two of your portfolio belongs in U.S. and international equities. A reasonable subdivision for this equity portion is two-thirds U.S. stocks and one-third international stocks. The distribution of world wealth actually suggests you should hold one-third in U.S. stocks and two-thirds in international. However, keeping a domestic bias toward the U.S. reflects the greater stability of U.S. markets and your own familiarity with U.S. versus foreign economies.

Do not hold more than 40 to 50 percent of your total investments in the first part of your portfolio. The reason is that the second part—equity investments—must provide most of the growth to replace the amount consumed from the first part. In other words, at an absolute minimum, you should keep at least 50 percent of your investment portfolio in stocks, whether you are a novice investor or a retiree.

This percentage flies in the face of much conventional investing wisdom. Many people are of the view that equities should decrease as you age, and they therefore use the 100-minus-your-age rule to determine stock allocation. The problem with this rule is that it breaks down in so many situations. If you are wealthy but elderly, for example, the rule is far too conservative. If you are not wealthy but young, with a lot of financial needs in the next decade, the rule is too aggressive. It makes much better sense to base your asset allocation on your need for the money.

I hear my female readers protest: "But Eleanor, I won't be retiring for at least fifteen years. Does this mean I should invest everything in equities?" My answer is that a retirement portfolio fully invested in equities can make good sense for younger investors. The long-term track record of the stock market is pretty robust, the recent economic meltdown notwithstanding. You are also likely adding to your portfolio regularly through annual or payroll contributions. This has the effect of diversifying your equity purchase price, which in turn protects you from investing only at the top of the market and reduces the risk of steep losses in a down market. Remember that you will begin to reduce your equity allocation, not on the date you start withdrawing money, but at least five to ten years before that.

You may still be dubious. "But Eleanor, what about my risk tolerance? Shouldn't that dictate my allocation to bonds and equities?" My answer again is no. I have always had reservations about the importance of risk tolerance when it comes to investing.

RISK TOLERANCE

Investment advisors and brokers often present new clients with questionnaires to try to determine their risk tolerance. These questionnaires generally fall into two categories. One focuses on the risk of different investments and asks the client to indicate her preference for one type of investment or another. For example, a client might be asked if she prefers aggressive growth to moderate growth, or she might be presented with various portfolios with different expected rates of return and possible losses and asked which she is most comfortable with. The second type of questionnaire focuses on the client and tries to elicit answers that will indicate whether she is a risk-taker by asking: "Do you wear a seat belt?" or "Have you ever gone bungee jumping?" or "Have you ever started a business?"

The problem with the first type is that the questions are apt to be poorly understood by those who do not understand investing in the first place, or who are not numerically fluent. The problem with the second is that risk-taking in the context of how we live, play, and work is poorly correlated with our attitudes toward investment risk. The most conservative investors I have ever met are small business owners, a huge proportion of whose businesses fail.

Risk tolerance is a chameleon—it changes with circumstances.

Risk tolerance is a chameleon—it changes with circumstances. In bull markets, most people feel confident about taking on risk and betting on equities because most bets are paying off. But when, say, the stock market loses 20 percent or more of its value, erstwhile risk-takers are few and far between. This is not a moral judgment on the fickleness of investors; it is simply an observation of human nature. Risk tolerance is very difficult to measure accurately because it depends on when someone is asked. It varies depending on the market backdrop and its outlook.

My final issue with risk tolerance is that, despite what people claim their tolerance to be, most people—women in particular—cannot afford the luxury of being intolerant to risk because it is the only way to earn higher returns. Only people like Bill Gates and Oprah Winfrey are exceptions. They have so much money that even if they decided to put their entire portfolio in gold bullion and keep it under the mattress, it would make very little difference to their lifestyles. For the rest of the world—which means you and me—a healthy proportion of higher-risk assets in our portfolios is necessary, both to grow our assets and to hedge against inflation.

Does this mean we should discard all notions of attitudes toward risk when it comes to investing? No. But I have found that the best way to understand how you really feel about risk is to identify your absolute bottom-line positions in extreme circumstances. What might make you decide to bail out of a given investment or to sell everything? What kinds of advice might be unacceptable to you? To understand your response to risk you must look at your past behavior. What did you do—if anything—with your investments during October 1987 when the market lost

23 percent? How were you investing in the late 1990s when dot-com stocks were all the rage? What were you thinking and doing in the final quarter of 2008 when the market was gripped with the worst financial crisis since the Great Depression?

If you are a new investor, looking at past behavior is not going to be of much help to you, but perhaps you have observed others in times of market extremes and developed some investment attitudes and expectations based on what you saw and felt. Vicarious experience can be a pretty powerful influence, as we know from dealing with the money beliefs of individuals whose parents lived through the Depression.

HOW DO WE INVEST?

In other words, we don't have to pore over investment charts or gaze at streaming stock tickers to be wise about investing.

We identified four markets to hold in your portfolio: cash in the form of money market instruments, U.S. bonds, U.S. stocks, and international stocks. We talked, too, about the long-term efficiency of those markets, which implies that there is no point for the individual investor to try to outsmart these markets through elaborate schemes of holding winning securities and avoiding the losers. In other words, we don't have to pore over investment charts or gaze at streaming stock tickers to be wise about investing.

But how do you hold a market? One way is to buy everything in it. In the case of U.S. stocks, that would mean buying every single publicly traded stock in proportion to its trading value in the overall stock market. Given the thousands of publicly traded stocks and our own limitations of time and money, however, this is not practical. If, however, we invest in a large pool of money that is in turn invested in most if not all U.S. stocks, we can participate in the stock market without expending vast sums of capital and computing power.

These pools of money are available in the form of funds called index mutual funds and exchange-traded funds (ETFs). Both are low-cost, convenient ways of investing designed to hold the same investments and produce the same performance as whatever market they are set up to track. There is no manager for these funds deciding which stocks to buy or sell; therefore, expenses are kept to a minimum. (And if you consider that managed mutual funds do worse than the market at least 50 percent of the time, this is not a liability, but a benefit.)

The rule of thumb, where you have a choice, is to use exchange-traded funds for large, discrete purchases and index funds for frequent, smaller purchases.

The performance of ETFs and index mutual funds tracking the same underlying index should be almost identical. So when would you buy one versus the other? One difference is that ETFs trade like stocks, so they may be bought and sold at any time during the day and can even be transacted with certain instructions, such as purchasing at a certain price.

Index mutual funds, by contrast, are bought and sold only at the closing prices at the end of the trading day. In my opinion, these trading differences are irrelevant to an investor who does not trade her account except to rebalance (which we will discuss shortly). However, cost differences can matter. Index mutual funds have annual expense costs that, while usually extremely low, are generally higher than their ETF counterparts. ETFs, by contrast, usually carry a transaction cost or ticket charge to buy or sell. The rule of thumb, where you have a choice, is to use ETFs for large, discrete purchases and index funds for frequent, smaller purchases.

Because we have kept our asset allocation simple, confined to four basic categories, we can keep our choice of ETFs or index funds relatively simple as well. Note, however, that these funds are available for stocks and bonds but not for cash. Money market investments are not commonly indexed. However, three categories of funds are available: prime money market funds (high-grade corporate instruments), government money market funds (U.S. Treasury securities and other agency short-term notes), and municipal money market funds. All are safe and highly regulated by the U.S. Securities and Exchange Commission, but I recommend going with a U.S. Treasury money market fund.

Table 6.1 lists the bond and stock markets that should be invested in, the indexes that track those markets, and examples of index funds and ETFs that replicate the indexes.

There are many other providers of index funds and ETFs, of course. You may find that the institution where you hold your investment account determines your available choices of ETFs or index funds. Some providers even have their own branded index funds or ETFs. What you need to ensure is that the funds you choose broadly represent the market you are attempting to hold.

Beware of specialty index funds or ETFs, which are becoming all the rage. Instead of tracking an entire market, these track particular aspects of a market or markets. For instance, there are index funds or ETFs that track banks or energy companies or gold companies. These funds have a very narrow focus and are, therefore, risky. When new flavors of index funds or ETFs become available in your 401(k) or 403(b) or fund family, do not

Table 6.1. Investment Possibilities

Market	Index	Index Description	Index Funds and ETFs
U.S. bonds	Barclay's Capital U.S. Aggregate Bond Index	Tracks total U.S. high-quality bond market. Includes government, corporate, and mortgage-backed bonds.	Vanguard Total Bond Market Index Fund iShares Barclays Aggregate Bond Fund
U.S. stocks	S&P 500	Tracks large U.S. companies.	Vanguard S&P 500 Index Fund
	Russell 3000	Tracks 3,000 U.S.-traded stocks.	iShares Russell 3000 Vanguard Total Stock Market VIPERS
	Wilshire 5000	Tracks over 7,000 U.S.-traded stocks.	Fidelity Spartan Total Market Index Fund Vanguard Total Stock Market Index Fund
International Stocks	MSCI EAFE Index	Tracks largest non-U.S. stocks in twenty-one developed countries.	Vanguard Developed Markets Index Fund iShares MSCI EAFE ETF

be tempted; stay the course with a broad whole-market exchange-traded or index fund. A new offering is worth considering only if it provides the same exposure you already have but at a lower expense. Otherwise, toss the fliers and brochures away with the credit card offerings. Better yet, shred them.

If you do decide that keeping it simple is not what you want for your portfolio, or you use an advisor who gets a bit fancier than suggesting mere market ETFs or index funds, consider maintaining a shadow keep-it-simple portfolio on paper as a benchmark to compare with your real portfolio. Periodically ask yourself or your advisor: "What would my results have been had we used market ETFs or indexes and cash? What would the expense differences have been? Is the complexity worth it?"

REBALANCING

To maintain the same asset allocation from year to year, you will have to rebalance your investments from time to time. There is strenuous debate among financial analysts as to the optimal frequency of rebalancing: whether it should be done at regular intervals or when triggered by events such as large moves in the underlying markets. Like so many other investing debates, this one has never been settled, so we will opt for the clearly practical (and proven) solution: rebalance annually.

You should reevaluate your portfolio every year. . . .

We have already discussed rebalancing to maintain a cash/bond reserve for the money you will need within the next five to ten years. You should reevaluate your portfolio every year to ensure you have the cash in place for the next year's withdrawals and for building another out-year of bond holdings to maintain the reserve horizon. Some of this money will need to be created by selling your equity funds and some will come from interest or cash dividend distributions. (If you are actively withdrawing from the portfolio, I recommend you do not reinvest your dividends, but let them accumulate in your money market reserve.)

Beyond this, you will also need to rebalance because of the differing performance of the markets you hold. Imagine, for instance, that you hold 40 percent of your portfolio in U.S. stocks and 20 percent in international stocks. If the international stocks increase in value but the U.S. stocks lose value in a particular year, the percentage of international stock in your portfolio may increase to 30 percent, with a corresponding decrease in the percentage of U.S. stocks. To reestablish the desired asset allocation in your portfolio, you may have to sell some international stocks and buy some U.S. stocks. You have probably heard the adage "buy low, sell high" as the key to success in investing. You may have also wondered (quite rightly) how to do this. One simple way is to rebalance as just described. You trim the winning asset classes and buy into the laggards. It works.

Your annual rebalancing review can be done at year-end, which also allows you to groom a taxable portfolio by taking tax losses. If you have holdings with unrealized capital losses in a taxable portfolio, you can sell these positions to create a tax loss to offset any other investment gains you may have for the year. Combine this grooming exercise with your rebalancing: sell the tax loss positions of a holding you need to trim for rebalancing reasons first. If you have tax losses in a position you do not need to trim, take these losses anyway and replace the position with an index fund or ETF similar, but not identical, to the one you are selling. Use a fund or ETF based on a different index of the broad market you hold. For example, if you sell an S&P 500 Index fund, replace the position with a Russell 3000 ETF. In this way, you will avoid running afoul of the IRS wash sale rules, which disallow the deduction of capital losses on positions you replace immediately.

TAXABLE VERSUS NONTAXABLE ACCOUNTS

Along with asset allocation, we should also consider asset location—specifically, which investments to keep in taxable versus nontaxable (or tax-deferred) accounts to achieve the highest after-tax returns.

The magic of tax-deferred compound growth, which you enjoy in your IRA or 401(k), works best over time with the highest-return assets, regardless whether that return is in the form of taxable income or an unrealized capital gain.

According to an old husbands' tale, you should put bonds in your tax-deferred retirement accounts and stocks in your taxable accounts for maximum tax benefits. Toss that one out, along with the notion that women can't invest. The magic of tax-deferred compound growth, which you enjoy in your IRA or 401(k), works best over time with the highest-return assets, regardless whether that return is in the form of taxable income or an unrealized capital gain. This suggests that we should put equity index funds or ETFs, which earn more in the long run, in the retirement accounts. Meanwhile, keeping cash and bonds in a taxable account means being able to get at your money if and when you need it without paying taxes for the privilege of using your own cash.

If you are tempted to stray from the simple investment approach I have advocated and start experimenting with individual stocks, don't put your stock experiment in your IRA. If you make mistakes—and you almost certainly will—allow yourself the government subsidy for your losses by keeping the stocks in your taxable account. Bear in mind, you can deduct up to $3,000 in capital losses over your gains on your tax return. Those beneficial losses would be denied you in your retirement account.

SOCIALLY RESPONSIBLE INVESTING

Some women will wonder how they can keep their investments simple and at the same time reconcile them with their social conscience. They prefer to invest only in those companies that demonstrate responsible corporate behavior. An increasing number of mutual funds, often referred to as ethical funds, have cropped up of late to capitalize on this investor desire. They purport to invest only in companies that do not violate moral principles about various issues, such as the environment, health, animal and human rights, or birth control, to name a few. Recent studies indicate that as much as 10 to 12 percent of managed investments are placed into so-called socially responsible companies.

My response is that social welfare and making money often make uncomfortable bedfellows. There is abundant evidence that socially conscious mutual funds have significantly underperformed funds in the broad, ethically unconstrained market over the long term. Furthermore, even an ethical mutual fund will charge you a higher management fee for the privilege of being selective about investing in certain companies. Meanwhile, the fund manager may not share all of your priorities. You could try investing directly in the stocks of socially responsible companies instead, but educating yourself would take a lot of digging on your part. You would need to establish such facts as the identity of the company's suppliers and customers, its hiring practices, its workplace procedures and policies, and so on. You would also need to monitor the companies in order to know if and when any of these factors changed.

As one of my clients explained: "I don't need the companies I invest in to care about the things that are important to me. I just need them to make me the money that will let me do my own caring."

Rather than trying to promote their values in the market, women should use the broad market as a means to preserve and grow their money, thus giving them the resources to pursue the values they really care about, including social values. As one of my clients explained: "I don't need the companies I invest in to care about the things that are important to me. I just need them to make me the money that will let me do my own caring."

THE INEVITABLE LURE OF STOCKS

Despite everything I have said, you will undoubtedly, at one time or another, succumb to the temptation to buy or hold a particular stock because you're sure you know something the rest of the world doesn't.

If I still haven't convinced you of the benefits of funds over individual stocks, consider the "sore thumb" argument. Imagine that a client comes to me for investment advice and I recommend index funds and ETFs to provide her with broad, low-expense exposure to equity markets, but she insists on holding one stock dear to her heart. She may have inherited it or bought it a long time ago, or her father may have worked for the company. In any event, she is attached to it and does not want to realize the tax gain by selling it, even though she has no intention of holding it until she dies. So we agree—me reluctantly and she eagerly—that we will allocate her portfolio around this stock for the time being. After all, it represents only a small part of her portfolio—maybe 3 or 4 percent.

We meet quarterly to discuss her investment results and talk occasionally on the phone. However, about half our conversation is taken up with the stock. Questions that commonly arise include: "What is the forecast for earnings? What are your thoughts on the shareholder lawsuit? What is the impact of the product recall?" She may even call me in a panic one day because the stock price has declined by 20 percent in a single week. Yet my suggestions to sell the stock are rebuffed.

Over time that one stock, which represents only a small part of the portfolio, becomes the sore thumb in her investment strategy. It sticks out and hurts disproportionately. It takes way too much time and attention relative to the other parts of the portfolio. The problem only intensifies when the number of single stocks owned goes up. You can end up with dozens of sore thumbs, all of them clamoring for attention, and at the same time you will find that each makes very little difference to your overall investment results.

What's so nice about stock funds is that individual stock activity is perceived by you only as gentle swells and dips in the background.

That is what's so nice about stock funds: all that individual stock activity is perceived by you only as gentle swells and dips in the background. Therefore, if you want a quiet (and relatively worry-free) life, hold funds, not stocks.

Decision Point ***Should I be investing in a 529 plan for my child's education?***

There are many financial planning tools and strategies named after sections in the Internal Revenue Code: 401(k) plans, 1031 like-kind exchanges, and 503(c)(3) organizations. A recently developed tool for saving for a child's post-secondary education is the 529 plan. Like its IRS cousins, the 529 plan offers distinct tax benefits. However, it requires careful attention to complex tax rules. Furthermore, 529 plans are not necessarily for everyone, nor do they provide a total solution to education savings.

These plans are established and administered by individual states, so every plan differs with respect to investment options, fees, and procedures for withdrawals. The following characteristics, however, are common to all 529 plans:

- Funds contributed to a 529 plan are not tax-deductible for federal taxes (although they may be for state taxes). The growth on these funds is exempt from taxes if used for qualified educational expenses.

- If funds are withdrawn from a 529 plan for non-educational purposes, the earnings on the funds become taxable and subject to a 10 percent penalty.

- A 529 plan is established for one beneficiary. If a parent or other individual is saving for more than one child, she or he should set up one plan for each child. It is possible, however, to redirect funds from one child's 529 to a sibling or other family member.

- A contribution to a 529 is considered a gift and is, therefore, subject to special gift and estate tax rules.

To determine whether you and your child are good candidates for a 529 plan, ask yourself the following questions:

- Is there sufficient time before my child enters college or other post-high school programs to get a real benefit from the tax deferral of plan earnings? The younger the child for whom the plan is established, the more powerful the effect of tax-free compounding. Also, the more time you have, the more aggressive your investments can be. For a child near college age, funds should generally be invested in conservative liquid instruments, such as short-term bonds and money market accounts. In such cases, the fees and complexity of a 529 plan may completely negate the benefit of tax-free returns.

- Have other education savings accounts been established and funded for my child? If the child already has funds for advanced education through a custodial account (known as an UGMA or UTMA account) or a trust, you may wish to reconsider adding yet another education account. Remember, the 529 plan can be used only for education costs without incurring a penalty.

- Have I made other gifts to my child? Contributions to a 529 plan count as a gift and are, therefore, part of the $13,000 per year/per donee exclusion from gift taxes and reporting. Thus, if you have made other gifts to the child in a given year, this could limit the amount you would want to contribute to a 529 plan. There is, however, a loophole for 529 plans that enables a donor to make the equivalent of five years' worth of gift tax exemptions in one year; however, this requires filing a special report with the IRS. It is also possible for a donor to split a gift to a 529 plan with his or her spouse, which allows a contribution of up to double the exemption amount, or $26,000 in a single year, or a one-time contribution of $130,000 to be spread over five years. Using this spreading technique means that any gifts made to the child in the subsequent four years after the initial contribution have to be added to the amount deemed contributed to the 529 in a given year for gift tax purposes.

CAN YOU RELATE?

I remember a cartoon in the financial press. The first frame shows a stock trader talking on the telephone, saying, "Okay, honey, talk to you later. Bye." In the next frame a nearby trader overhears this conversation, perks up, and repeats what he has just heard: "Buy?" Next, dozens of frenzied traders are running around, shouting: "Buy! Buy! Buy!" Meanwhile the original trader stands at the edge of the fray, unaware of what is going on and, still talking on the phone, says: "Yeah. Okay. G'bye. Give me a call later on my cell." This last word, too, gets picked up by the traders and by the last frame they are all screaming: "Sell! Sell! Sell!"

- Is it likely that my child is eligible for financial aid or a grant or scholarship? Unlike a custodial account, which is considered the child's asset and thereby offsets the financial aid for which a child might be eligible, a 529 plan is considered the owner's asset. If the owner is a parent, a percentage of the 529 plan is deemed to be available to the child. If the owner is a grandparent, there is no impact on the amount of eligible aid; however, once distributions begin from the 529 plan, they are considered nontaxable income to the child, which can disqualify or limit the amount of financial support based on need.

- Last, but not least in importance, is a question that few people take time to consider: Is the tax-free growth of a 529 worth it to me? If you are in a low income tax bracket or have special circumstances that might result in no or very low taxes, the value of the tax-free growth within the 529 may not be significant to you. Consider, too, that the nontaxable growth comes at a cost, namely, the complexity of these plans and the loss of control you have over contributed assets.

CAN YOU RELATE?

Consider this: you are about to set off to the beach on a holiday weekend, and the traffic guy on the local news station advises that the best time to travel to the beach is between 7 and 9 a.m. Do you follow his advice, or do you instead think: "Well, now that he's told everyone to leave at 7 a.m., that is going to be the worst time, not the best!" If you think along these lines, the idea of market efficiency—namely a market where there's no way to beat the traffic—will make perfect sense to you.

Clearly, the rules that govern 529s make these plans less attractive for the faint of heart. You have to take a lot of factors into account when investing in these vehicles. I recommend that you talk to a financial professional to help you navigate through the plan and the various investment options it presents. If you feel confident to do it yourself, the best website on 529 plans is www.savingforcollege.com. It was created by the undisputed expert on these plans, Joseph Hurley, who has also written *the* book on the subject: *The Best Way to Save for College: A Complete Guide to 529 Plans*, now in its eighth edition.

Once you've cleared a path through the information weeds on 529 plans, you can keep it pretty simple by following some of the common-sense recommendations I always offer my clients:

- Do not try to do all your college funding in a 529 plan. Diversification is just as important here as elsewhere. Put aside some savings in your own name to retain control and flexibility. Consider whether it is going to be possible for you to pay for some of your child's tuition out-of-pocket. The advantage is that if you pay the college or university directly, the tuition portion is not considered a gift for tax purposes and does not replace other gifts you may wish to make to your child.

- Obtain a low-expense plan. To be more specific, look for state plans sponsored by Vanguard or TIAA-CREF. Keeping expenses low is as important as taking advantage of tax-free growth. Do not throw away the tax benefit by paying too much in fees.

- Avoid plans that automatically rebalance from stocks to bonds, particularly in the last couple of years before withdrawals from the plan are about to be made. I agree with the premise that you need to have less volatile holdings as you get closer to withdrawal, but bear markets in bonds have been known to happen and can be quite devastating. Invest in cash instead. It is much cheaper as an investment option, and you will want the liquidity of cash as you come close to making tuition payments.

CAN YOU RELATE? (I HOPE NOT!)

Authors Ori and Rom Brafman, in the book Sway: The Irresistible Pull of Irrational Behavior, *give an example of rational people behaving irrationally. They describe a classroom exercise used by a Harvard Business School professor. It involves auctioning a $20 bill under the following rules. Everyone can participate and bids must proceed in increments of $1. When the bidding ends, the top bidder gets the bill. Here's the catch, however. The next closest bidder not only loses the auction, but has to pay in her or his last bid.*

At first there are lots of bidders, but then as the bidding approaches $20, people start pulling out. Inevitably, two people remain. As the bidding continues to rise, the second-place person becomes determined not to be the sucker who pays good money for nothing in return. As a result, the auction usually continues well past the $20 point, sometimes to as high as over $200. As the Brafmans explain, people are determined not to lose. As a result, "The deeper the hole they dig themselves into, the more they continue to dig."

SUGGESTED ROUTES

www.etfdesk.com
A good resource for locating and screening exchange-traded funds.

www.investopedia.com
This popular investment education website provides a comprehensive glossary to investment terms and phrases. Investopedia also offers a stock simulator to set up a mock portfolio and track your success (or lack thereof) in buying and selling individual stocks.

www.morningstar.com
The preeminent source for mutual fund data, Morningstar also features information on ETFs and individual stocks. Morningstar offers two membership levels: free, and a premium subscription that allows in-depth research on investment options and provides tools to manage your portfolio.

Bogle, John C. *Bogle on Mutual Funds: New Perspectives for the Intelligent Investor*, Dell Publishing, 1994.

Ellis, Charles D. *Winning the Loser's Game: Timeless Strategies for Successful Investing*, McGraw–Hill, 2009.

Malkiel, Burton G. *A Random Walk Down Wall Street*, W.W. Norton & Co., 2003.

Chapter Seven

Women Plan—Retirement and the New Reality

Not long ago, retirement was popularly perceived as the golden pond, a serene interlude untroubled by financial worry or risk. It was a time when your working life drew to a close and you reaped the rewards of your toil, a time when you put your feet up and your biggest worry was whether to shop, golf, or visit the grandkids.

This vision of retirement as a risk-free, care-free permanent vacation is attributable to the type of pension plan that was most commonly provided up until the 1980s, particularly by government and large corporations: defined benefit plans. Under these plans, retirees were paid a fixed amount of money on a regular basis based on a predetermined formula. The benefits under these plans were generous and predictable, and not subject to the ups and downs of the market. Retirees did not have to trouble themselves with investment choices, asset allocation, or rebalancing. These concerns belonged only to the pension provider. As long as the monthly check arrived on time, all was well in the retiree's world.

The popularity of these pension plans began a sharp descent in the 1980s. The causes were many, not least of which was the excessive cost to companies due to increased life expectancies and changing accounting standards. These shifts, in turn, led to changes in retirement statutes and regulations governing the plans.

Many companies began eliminating defined benefit plans and replaced them with defined contribution plans through 401(k)s and profit-sharing plans. The primary benefits for these companies were reduced costs and reduced risk. Instead of a pooled plan for all employees, each employee was given his own account for investment in the market. The downside for the employee, of course, was that she assumed the risk previously borne by the company. Her benefits upon retirement depended on her choice of investments and how they have performed.

The individual retirement account, or IRA, also made its appearance during this period, providing retirement savers a tax-advantaged way to save on their own if they did not have access to company plans or they wished to supplement their company's plans. Like their 401(k) counterparts, self-directed IRAs put all the decision-making authority in the hands of the account holder. Retirees were popped into the driver's seat of their own retirement vehicle, even when many of them had no real idea how to operate it.

This proliferation of self-directed retirement accounts was a bonanza for stockbrokers and investment advisors. Throughout the 1980s and 1990s, advice on retirement plan management was in high demand by individuals, particularly baby boomers, who didn't have the first clue about how to plan and invest for retirement. Fortunately—and to some extent as a result of this interest in investing—the stock market rallied substantially, interrupted only by the popping of the tech bubble in 2000 to 2002. The booming stock market also coincided with a housing boom fueled by low interest rates. People began to feel quite confident about taking on responsibility for their own investments. Everyone was feeling asset-rich, and few people were worrying about whether they would have enough to retire on. If their spending was out of hand, it could all be fixed by a few good years of double-digit returns in the market.

This all changed with the economic meltdown that reached its crisis in 2008 and 2009. Within a short period of time, the value of many people's homes—perhaps the biggest and most visible emblems of their affluence—declined by as much as 30 to 40 percent. Estimates say half of American homeowners will be left with negative home equity by 2011. A vicious cycle was perpetuated when consumer despair about their ability to meet their mortgages spread to the stock market. A further $2 trillion vanished from Americans' retirement savings.

Recently, many have begun to realize that they haven't saved enough for their longevity, and what they have accumulated has taken a near knockout punch.

Baby boomers are now finding themselves on the verge of older age, but no longer on the verge of being able to retire. As long-haired youths they preached free love. As buttoned-down adults they practiced free spending. They always assumed they would live forever, but now longevity is looking like a double-edged sword. Recently, many have begun to realize that they haven't saved enough for their longevity, and what they have accumulated has taken a near knockout punch. Clearly it is time to retire the conventional notions of retirement.

THE FEMALE PERSPECTIVE

Many female baby boomers, in particular, are feeling the sting of reduced asset values. Due to the various factors we have discussed, women often arrive at the last third of their lives well behind their male counterparts in terms of financial readiness.

Employers need to take equal pay for equal work seriously, not only because it is good ethics, but because it is good management. Paying women what they are worth and addressing their particular needs for work-family balance will result in higher workplace satisfaction, which in turn leads to higher productivity and profits. Legislation could also go some way to remedying the inherent handicap women face in saving for retirement, such as giving social security earnings credit for the important but unpaid work done by stay-at-home mothers or caretakers. We have also discussed what women can do for themselves to close the income and asset gap with men—spend less, earn more, and get more aggressive about investing the difference.

But while many women may start the race toward retirement security at a significant disadvantage, once there they may be better suited to deal with the new, rapidly evolving retirement reality than their male counterparts. Thriving in retirement can be less about what we have and more about what we do. In many ways, this plays to women's strengths: their ability to take on and balance different and simultaneous roles, their penchant for planning—and, yes, their propensity to worry.

Retirement is so often something we plan to plan for.

Obviously, many people are not financially ready to retire today because they did not worry enough. What's important, however, is that women translate their worry into awareness and action. Planning is the key and it must be done *now*. Retirement is so often something we plan to plan for, with the result that it isn't until most people are in their fifties that they seriously start to think about what their retired lives might look like.

THE FOUR PERCENT RULE

Let's start with the most basic question: What does a financially successful retirement look like? For years, the answer was thought to be a certain amount of money you needed to accumulate: some experts said that this amount was $1 million, while others recommended even more as a result of rapidly escalating health care costs. Financial advisor Bill Bengen looked at this question another way, not as a problem of accumulation, but as one of making whatever you had accumulated last for your lifetime. In his research he set out to determine what rate of withdrawal from a retirement portfolio would avoid the problem of running out. Bengen looked at actual stock returns and retirement scenarios over the previous seventy-five years, and found that retirees who draw-down 4.2 percent or less of their portfolio in the initial year, then adjust that amount every subsequent year for inflation, stand a good chance that their money will outlive them. This formula is often referred to as the "Four Percent Rule."

Subsequent studies have supported this rule. Using actual historical data as well as randomized data, these studies have confirmed that this rule stands up in situations as chaotic and grim as normal investment markets can sometimes be. The four percent rate is, therefore, often considered an optimized rate; in other words, it is the highest annual rate of withdrawal you can make under various conditions of uncertainty, such as extended bear markets or periods of inflation, without running out of money for periods of up to thirty years.

Bengen's analysis also showed that the difference between success and failure is not that great. He found that retirees who took 5 percent a year from their portfolios ran a 30 percent chance that their nest eggs would run out of steam before they did. Those who took 6 to 7 percent would face a greater than 50 percent chance of running out of money before they died.

For those of us who don't have the know-how or discipline to implement the Four Percent Rule on our own, the financial world has created a variety of vehicles to help us manage a sustainable withdrawal rate.

For those of us who don't have the know-how or discipline to implement the Four Percent Rule on our own, the financial world has created a variety of vehicles to help us manage a sustainable withdrawal rate. As is so often the case, unfortunately, the proliferation of these products and services in the marketplace only contributes to confusion for the average consumer. Table 7.1 sets out a comparison of the four basic types of products and services, broadly described as retirement income solutions, that can assist you in managing retirement withdrawals.

EXERCISE 7–1. WHAT MATTERS TO YOU?

Based on Bengen's analysis, the amount you need to retire is roughly twenty-five times what you expect to spend each year. But there is no universal agreement about the magic retirement number—the amount of wealth you have to accumulate to be free of the necessity of working. This is probably because, to some degree, the number is individual to the person retiring and his or her circumstances.

Whatever number is considered adequate to retire on, the more important question for many is this: How do I get there? Try to imagine what your retirement might look like. If this picture is not coming to you, think about someone you know who is retired. Now try to identify what in your estimation are the most important factors that will determine your (or his or her) ability to be financially independent.

Table 7.1. Comparison of Retirement Income Solutions

	Annuities	Retirement Income Pay-out Funds	Target Date Funds/Life Cycle Funds	Working with an Advisor
Description	Contract with insurance company; for given amount, purchaser receives promise of periodic payments for life or specific period of time	Mutual funds designed to provide monthly or periodic income for fixed period or life	Mutual funds that provide income and adjust asset allocation to lower risk as target date approaches	Personal advisor assists clients to accumulate funds for retirement, manage spending in retirement, and manage allocation and draw-down of investments
Differentiating Features	Variable vs. fixed (amount of payments) Deferred vs. immediate (when payments begin)	Payments consist of principal vs. income only Payments for a fixed period vs. payments for life	Target dates usually in five-year increments, range from 2010 to 2050 Different funds use different glide paths; i.e., allocation changes over time to reduce equity risk	Advisor may provide financial planning as well as investment management, or investment management only

(continued)

Table 7.1. *(continued)*

	Annuities	**Retirement Income Pay-out Funds**	**Target Date Funds/Life Cycle Funds**	**Working with an Advisor**
Differentiating Features, con't	Life vs. certain period (payments received for life or for fixed period of time) Single vs. joint life (payments over one or two lifetimes)	Level of payout for lifetime funds range from 3 to 7 percent annually	Stock allocation at target rate ranges from 40 to 60 percent Expense ratios range from 0.19 percent (Vanguard) to above 2 percent	Methods of compensation: percentage of assets under management; flat fee; fee plus commission; wrap fee Advice may be subject to minimum account sizes (e.g., $1 million)
Pros	Provide income for life Can be used to transfer investment risk to the insurance company	Simplifies management of portfolio to provide predictable and/or sustainable income over extended period of time	Simplifies process of modifying asset allocation over long periods of time	Most responsive to individual needs and contingencies Best suited where ongoing counsel on spending may be needed

	Some annuities carry guarantees of contract value, payment amount, or return of premium		Intended to avoid problem of severe decline in market coinciding with need for funds	
Cons	Contractual provisions can be complex Complicated fee/expense structure (mortality expenses, surrender charges, management fees for variable contracts) Total expense to annuity holder can be high Generally illiquid (cannot get all money out of contract without surrender fees in first years)	Payouts not guaranteed Products are new, thus unproven to deliver on promoted benefits Allocation to equities in some funds may be too low given time period and need for growth	Not a solution for providing retirement income While designed to lower risk as investor nears retirement, a bear market in bonds at or near retirement date could defeat funds' purpose One size (date) made to fit all; convenience, rather than performance, is chief attribute	Minimum account size may put advisory relationship above the reach of less affluent clients

(continued)

Table 7.1. *(continued)*

	Annuities	Retirement Income Pay-out Funds	Target Date Funds/Life Cycle Funds	Working with an Advisor
Cons, con't	Early death, in contract without guaranteed death benefits, could result in loss of investment			
Recommendations	Consider using fixed annuity as part (up to 25 percent) of retirement portfolio Variable annuity best used for accumulating funds for retirement if other retirement savings vehicles (401(k); IRAs) are maxed out	Consider using as part of a retirement portfolio to simplify process of regular income generation, particularly if not using an advisor for this purpose	Use only in cases where portfolio would not otherwise be rebalanced over time and/or where convenience/ simplicity is paramount	If affordable, this is best solution for managing finances (investments, spending, estate planning) during retirement

		May be well suited as way to provide income to a beneficiary or spouse as a trust replacement	Choose only low-expense funds offered by premier fund families: Vanguard, Fidelity, T. Rowe Price Have a plan in place, or get advice, when target date is reached and funds are distributed	Use advisor to help with decisions on other retirement solutions: annuities, pay-out funds, target date funds; however, discuss with advisor any fee redundancy that might result (e.g., advisory fee on top of annuity fee)

Once you have compiled this list, rank the factors in order of importance. The following are critical in my view. How many of the following did your list include?

- Annual amount saved for retirement
- Asset allocation of retirement portfolio
- Proportion of savings in retirement versus non-retirement accounts
- Market performance while saving for retirement
- Years of savings
- Date of retirement
- Market performance while living in retirement
- Debt burden before and after retirement
- Expense management before and after retirement
- Taxes/tax rates
- Inflation
- Longevity
- State of health
- Health costs

Now go through your list and rank each factor in order of what worries you the most (hint: this is likely to be identical or similar to your importance list). Then go through the list and assign to each factor one of the following: "C" = I can control this factor; "NC" = I have no control; or "SC" = I have at least some control.

You can see from the number of items on the list that an awful lot of variables go into determining a successful retirement. The key is to first focus on the most important variables, and then on those that can be controlled.

Not every person will regard the same factors as controllable. For instance, I usually consider debt burden, years of savings, and date of retirement as controllable, but a woman with excessive debt or a disability may not. For those variables that cannot be controlled, the best approach is to use some conservative but reasonable assumptions. These typically include (but may not be limited to) the following:

- Market performance before and after retirement (it might be reasonable to assume an 8 percent annual return for stocks and 4 percent for bonds)
- Tax rates (assume a 25 percent average rate)
- Inflation (assume 3 percent)
- Longevity (assume you will live to age ninety-five)
- Health costs (assume $150,000 to $200,000 of out-of-pocket costs in retirement)

Successful retirement planning is about being proactive when it comes to the important variables we can control, either completely or at least in part. For instance, although health care costs are beyond your control—many, in fact, see them as out of control—you do have some ability to keep them in check by the lifestyle choices you make. Most of us don't regard staying fit and healthy as part of a strategy to ensure a successful retirement—but we should. Inflation and taxes, too, are often considered acts of God or, at least, acts of out-of-reach legislators and Federal Reserve chairmen, but we can still make consumption and investment choices to limit their impact on our retirement.

The younger we are, the more control we have. Unfortunately, it is precisely when we're young that we feel least able and motivated to plan for retirement. Student loans, credit card debt, a first home, and the expenses of rearing and educating children all take priority. This probably explains why, according to Department of Labor statistics, fewer than half of employed women in this country participate in their employers' retirement plans. The pressures of now keep crowding out the needs of later. But we take back control if we heed those financial industry ads that illustrate the exponential benefits of saving for retirement sooner rather than later.

Maximizing the positive impact of the factors we can control sometimes takes research. Take the variable that many people believe is the key to retirement success: asset allocation, or what you choose to invest in. There is no disputing the wisdom that a young woman saving for retirement should allocate a significant percentage of her funds to stocks—as much as 100 percent in her twenties and 80 percent or more even up to age fifty. These hefty allocations provide the necessary growth while the investor still has sufficient time to recover from greater losses risked with equities. However, opinion differs on the appropriate stock allocation after retirement, when withdrawals begin.

Fear causes many people to think that they must radically reduce their equity exposure and hide out primarily in bonds or other safe income-producing securities once they enter retirement.

Fear causes many people to think that they must radically reduce their equity exposure and hide out primarily in bonds or other safe income-producing securities once they enter retirement. Some still have the voices of their Depression-bred parents ringing in their ears: "Don't risk losing your principal. Invest for income." There is also a persistent adage that the right percentage to hold in stocks is determined by taking the number one hundred and subtracting your age. My usual response to this is: "So I guess that means when you hit your 101st birthday, you'll have to start shorting stocks!" (Shorting is a strategy whereby you borrow stocks to sell them, which effectively means your stock allocation is negative.) In other words, I do not hold this rule of thumb in very high regard.

The best answer to what percentage of stock you should hold in retirement is somewhat counterintuitive, but supported by research. The analytical work done by retirement withdrawal expert Bill Bengen also provides some guidance in this area. Bengen found that a portfolio must remain at least 50 percent invested in stocks to be sustainable at the 4 percent rate. But, surprisingly, he also found there was very little difference to portfolio longevity between those invested 50 percent in stock and those invested in as much as 75 percent stock.

Consider all those investors who spend money, not to mention time, choosing investment products or advisors to try to achieve what they believe is the magic mix of stocks and bonds that will perpetuate their retirement fund. What Bengen's research shows is that once you have a healthy percentage to begin with, a 15 or even 25 percent change in stock allocation is no more than a cosmetic touch.

FLEXIBILITY IS THE KEY

In my experience, the single most important factor that determines a successful retirement—and fortunately one we can control—is living within your means. It doesn't matter whether you retire on $10 million, on $100,000, or on social security. It doesn't matter whether you're single, divorced, or married. If you can maintain your spending within your financial circumstances, you will succeed.

This is not just a matter of exercising sufficient will or being on a constant financial diet. The ability to live within your means requires being flexible and adaptable in different financial circumstances. This, in turn, requires keeping your fixed expenses, such as debt payments, to a minimum. It sometimes also calls for unorthodox solutions, such as increasing your means by going back to work when times are tough. Most important, it means timing inevitable expenses strategically so they will do the least damage to your reserves.

When returns are down, retirees should reduce their expenses and/or delay certain expenditures. Conversely, when returns are up, retirees can spend more. In this regard, the simple Four Percent Rule is instructive as a guideline but may be unrealistic in practice. Rarely, if ever, can we, or should we, spend the same amount of money each year. Some necessary expenses are inevitably large, lumpy, and irregular: a new roof, for instance, or a car.

The following simple math illustrates the importance of this point. If your investment account loses 10 percent, it will take an 11.1 percent gain to get back to even. If, in addition to the 10 percent loss, you take an additional 2 percent out of your account because it's time to buy a new car, you now have to make 13.6 percent to get the account back to even. Delaying this expenditure until a year when the investment account has gains to absorb the withdrawal can make the retirement road much smoother. Furthermore, as mothers also know, sometimes putting off an expenditure eliminates its apparent necessity.

Typical retirement saving and spending plans offered on the internet or by planners using basic software packages do not always prepare retirees for these contingencies. Many plans use straight-line projections of returns and fail to take into account the variability of returns around an expected average. Consider this important difference: while two retirees may both earn an average 8 percent annual return for twenty years, one achieves this average by earning 8 percent year in and year out, while the other enjoys some years where her return is well above the average 8 percent and endures other years where it is far below, even negative. The financial security of the second retiree will be more precarious than that of the first, but also closer to the truth.

To capture this reality, many plans now build in probability measures, such that you are given a percentage likelihood of not running out of money rather than a blunt "yes" or "no" answer to the "Can I retire?" question. Suppose you are told you have a 60 percent probability of not running out of money. Should you not like these odds, the plan then usually proposes a one-time fix: increase your savings from $2,500 to $4,000 a year for twenty years, for instance, or reduce spending over the next twenty-five years from $6,000 a month to $4,500 a month, or increase your stock allocation from 35 percent to 60 percent. However, even these recommendations quickly lose their relevance over time as circumstances continue to change.

What is missing from most retirement projections is *if/then* guidance to deal with life's inevitable twists and turns. Instead of static, long-term projections, what pre-retirees and retirees need is a retirement simulator that teaches them how to make mid-course corrections, similar to the way flight simulators are used to teach pilots how to react to the changing conditions of flying. Until such a tool is developed, the best alternative, if you are having difficulty responding to changing circumstances, is to get input from a financial planner. The planner's advice, however, should be directional rather than definitive, and should build in plenty of potential detours and alternative routes.

TAX CONSIDERATIONS

No chapter on retirement planning would be complete, of course, without a brief discussion about tax considerations. It is important to maximize your retirement savings, which usually means accumulating these savings in a tax-deferred 401(k) or rollover IRA. While I agree that you should first contribute to these accounts up to the maximum amount allowable, I also advocate setting aside additional money in one or more savings or investment accounts. Any income in these types of account is taxed, but once it is time to take money out, a substantial portion can be withdrawn tax-free, unlike your withdrawals from your IRA or 401(k).

Most people arrive in retirement with just two major assets: their house and their tax-deferred retirement plan. This may provide them a net worth that can support an average annual 4 percent withdrawal, inflation-adjusted, for thirty to thirty-five years, but they may find themselves painted into a tax corner: every dollar they need for their expenses has to be grossed up for taxes, which may be higher than they formerly were as a result of decreasing deductions (e.g., mortgage interest) or fewer personal exemptions. Suppose a retired couple needs to buy a car. The $40,000 cost may require a $50,000 withdrawal from the IRA account due to taxes. They might instead tap the equity in their home through a line of credit, but the funds for paying the loan, assuming they come from the IRA, will also be subject to tax.

I often tell my clients that the period between ages 59½ and 70½ can be a sweet spot for creative tax planning. During this time, you are exempt from the "too early, too late, too little, or too much" tax rules that otherwise pertain to withdrawals from your IRAs. During this time you can take money from your retirement accounts without any early withdrawal penalty, but you are not required to. This can provide you with enormous flexibility if you have taxable accounts in addition to 401(k) and/or IRA accounts.

By having a choice as to where you can go to get your needed cash flow—from either the pretax or after-tax accounts—you can fine-tune the amount of taxable income you provide yourself each year in a way that was not possible while you were earning a regular income. You can bunch taxable income in one year and nontaxable in another, depending on the amounts of your deductions, credits, or social security benefits. So if, for example, you need a new car and a withdrawal from the IRA would increase your taxable income and put you over certain thresholds for deductions, you can simply draw from your already-taxed account for the car funds and thereby avoid the extra taxes.

Some of my retired clients in their sixties have even been able to get their taxable income low enough to permit a rollover from their traditional IRAs into a Roth IRA at a very low tax bracket. They draw just enough from the taxable IRA to come within the 15 percent tax bracket, then set aside these funds in a Roth account where they can later be drawn upon tax-free.

These strategies are, of course, highly dependent on getting all your income, deduction, and cash flow planets to line up for a perfect tax eclipse, and this takes thoughtful coordination and consultation with a tax or financial advisor. But the general point remains: you cannot even consider such strategies without first having diversified your retirement resources between taxable and tax-deferred savings.

Saving money for retirement over and above your tax-deferred retirement account is also recommended as an obvious, but rarely utilized, way to build your retirement funds. Ideally, I recommend saving an additional 10 percent or more of your wages or employment income—so if you think your take-home pay is all yours, think again. Before taking that paycheck home, stop at the bank or the brokerage and make a deposit to an after-tax account.

This recommendation is particularly urgent for women, who often have so much catching up to do in compiling an adequate retirement portfolio. I have cited the hurdles faced by women, but they bear repeating: the wage gap, fewer years in the workforce, and longer lives. These all result in the average woman needing to save considerably more than a man. Because the amount she can save in her 401(k) is limited by her (usually) lower wages, she must look to non-retirement accounts as a way of saving more.

RETIREMENT: A NEW BEGINNING

For those who have failed to prepare properly for retirement, working longer will become a necessity. A subset of older people will continue working to obtain health care benefits, especially if they retire from their trade or profession before age sixty-five, when they become eligible for Medicare. Like street people who "Will Work for Food," these seniors "Will Work for Benefits." Because they are older, they invariably have a chronic condition or two that makes getting individual health insurance difficult, frustrating, and very expensive. The lure of a group policy where bad knees and high cholesterol can disappear in a large risk pool is strong enough to get them rising with an alarm clock again. One of my more enterprising clients took a job as a crossing guard with the local school system, while another drove a bus for a nursing home just a few years before he himself became a resident there.

Even those who have saved enough to retire are continuing to work.

Even those who have saved enough to retire are continuing to work. They are choosing to stay active for various reasons, and often earning an income is just one of the benefits. Ideally, they have more choices about the type of work they do and how and where they do it than they did when they were younger. Their choices are based less on the need to buy houses, educate children, and pay for divorces and more on who they are and how they want to spend their increasingly precious time.

The trend among baby boomers to have children later in life has meant that many are still actively parenting in their fifties. Some have discovered that it may be more important and rewarding to stay home with their kids when they are teenagers as opposed to when they are infants or toddlers. The result is that many consider an early retirement or sabbatical to cover this period until their children leave home, at which point they will resume their careers or start a new one. Author and newspaper columnist Abigail Trafford celebrates this period in her book *My Time*, sharing stories of individuals who start new projects and adventures in their "retirement" that simply would not have been feasible for their parents.

Retirement, in short, is a concept that is changing, both due to necessity and choice. It is no longer just a time when people leave the workforce and put their feet up, but a time when many are redirecting their energies and activities. Indeed, books on retirement have suggested that the word *retiring* has become outdated and needs to be replaced with words like *rewiring* or *retooling*. They suggest that retirement does not signal an end, but a new beginning.

Circling In on Reinvention

Hire your friends as your advisory board for your own retirement reinvention enterprise. Share with them your vision and mission for the life you will live in retirement. Use them as a sounding board to help you both dream and be practical about changing careers, for instance, or starting a new business. They can also hold you accountable to your plan, and help you as you face the inevitable challenges and opportunities.

This change in attitude is in large part thanks to our longer, healthier lives. There is no doubt that modern medicine and life-styles have paid big dividends in terms of longevity. Not long ago, people would have ten years at most to look forward to in retirement. Now the fastest growing segment of the American population is the cohort of those ninety years or older, referred to as the "oldest old."

Choosing to think about retirement in this different way is imperative for most women, for whom a longer retirement is more likely. Seeing it not as a number—not purely as an obligation that you have to fund—but as a time for redirecting and rechanneling your lifetime skills, can transform what is otherwise an anxiety-laden unknown into something that can be happily anticipated and creatively planned.

I am personally in favor of a word such as "retiming" instead of retiring, convinced that retirement is significantly and profoundly concerned with our changing sense and use of time.

I am personally in favor of a word such as "retiming" instead of retiring, convinced that retirement is significantly and profoundly concerned with our changing sense and use of time. We often think of retirement as being all about managing money—one scarce resource—when in fact it is also just as importantly about managing time—another, even scarcer resource. I remember as a thirty-year-old being told by an office colleague who was twice my age that the older you got, the faster time would pass. It was a scary thought to me. I was already frantic trying to pack all I had to do as a young mother, graduate student, and employee into my too-short days. How could life go any faster? Fast-forward twenty years, and I know my colleague had it absolutely right.

We can die with money left over, but the balance in our time accounts always hits zero. Perhaps in planning for a good retirement we all need to make a much bigger deal of this stubborn fact. I have to say this to myself as much and as often as I do to you, my female readers and clients. We generally think we do well by advising to save, save, save. But when it comes to time as opposed to money, we need to tell ourselves and others to spend as if there were no tomorrow.

Decision Point ***Should I be investing for my retirement before saving for my children's education?***

> *Most financial advisors advocate saving for retirement before funding education. Their reasons are several. You cannot borrow money for retirement in the same way you can for college. Federal retirement loans have not yet been invented (although given the amount of federal stimulus to help markets recover from the 2008 financial crisis, such loans may well be next on the drawing board). Students, on the other hand, enjoy a special status in that they do not have to have money to get money. Tax advantages are another reason advisors are in favor of saving for retirement first. Failing to put money into your retirement plan at work, particularly when your employer is matching your contribution, or not taking advantage of the tax deduction for an IRA if you are eligible, is like stepping over a big pile of cash on the sidewalk. While there are some tax credits or deductions for college savings, the savings are generally small relative to the tax benefits of retirement plans.*

These arguments are pretty compelling and I have certainly been known to cite them. I have also found, however, that putting retirement savings ahead of education savings does not necessarily sit well with some women, even those who are well aware of the financial benefits. What it comes down to, in their minds, is a choice between their children's welfare and their own. It may be un-American not to try to save on taxes, but they consider it outright unnatural not to provide for their children.

The timing of education costs versus retirement also comes into play. Usually our kids go to college before we retire (though with the trend of delaying children into our forties, this is becoming less so). Therefore, putting money aside for education often seems more urgent because it is more proximate. Retirement also costs much more than four years of college. As a result, college may seem easier (and even more satisfying) to fund.

CAN YOU RELATE?

A study published in 2008 by The Hartford Financial Services Group and MITAge Lab looked at the differences in the way men and women view retirement. Not surprisingly, women worry much more than men about issues that affect their financial security, such as inflation, health care costs, and longevity. However, there was one retirement challenge that women face more confidently than men: the question of what they will do in retirement.

While there may be a right financial answer to the question, the choice to fund retirement or children's education first will depend on the individual. This issue is similar to the question as to whether a young adult should pay off all her credit card debt before investing in a retirement plan. The financial answer is clear: get rid of the debt first. But to many, paying off debt feels less effective. If you are one of those who feel compelled to fund education before retirement, my advice is that doing some of both is better than doing all of one and none of the other.

Here are my rules for saving for retirement and your children's education—to be gently broken as your personal circumstances dictate:

- If your employer offers a match on your contributions to a retirement plan, contribute at least up to the match. Make this a priority over education savings, if you can.

- If you are eligible for a deductible IRA, fund the IRA up to the allowable limit. To allay any guilt you might feel about putting money into the IRA rather than a college account, consider that you are generally allowed to withdraw money from this IRA for education costs without incurring an early distribution penalty; 401(k) and 403(b) plans also allow participants to borrow money for education without an early withdrawal penalty, although interest is charged and the money must be repaid within five years.

- Use tax-qualified vehicles for education savings—that is, 529 plans (see page 137). These plans work similarly to retirement plans in that the investments grow tax-free. Unlike retirement plans, however, contributions to 529 plans are not deductible for federal income taxes. On the other hand, withdrawals are tax-free if used for qualified education expenses.

- Do not try to fund education costs completely with 529s. Keep some of the savings for college in a taxable account in your own name. You may forgo some tax benefits, but you gain autonomy and flexibility. This account could also be considered a vehicle both for education and retirement savings.

CAN YOU RELATE?

I met with Susan Bradley, CFP®, founder of the Sudden Money Institute, to talk about women and retirement. According to Susan, life's transitions, such as retirement, are about temporarily losing your footing, moving through and then away from crisis toward solution. She believes that women often navigate this transition better than men because they are accustomed to situations where they don't have all the answers. "Women are okay not knowing," says Susan. They can deal with the ambiguity of an uncertain future.

SUGGESTED ROUTES

www.dol.gov/ebsa/publications/women.html

This Department of Labor page, "Women and Retirement Savings," discusses why the retirement savings gap is so great for women and recommends ways to make the best use of employer-sponsored plans, social security benefits, and your own savings (IRAs and simple plans).

www.thetransitionnetwork.org

The Transition Network is a community of women over age fifty who support one another as they make the transition from one career to another or to the next phase of their lives.

www.troweprice.com
T. Rowe Price is a highly respected mutual fund company dedicated to the education and success of its investors. On this website, you can navigate to the "Individual Investors" section through to a tool called "Retirement Income Calculator." Use this tool to model and understand the factors that will increase the likelihood of your retirement success.

Trafford, Abigail. *My Time: Making the Most of the Bonus Decades After 50*, Perseus Publishing, 2003.

Chapter Eight

Women Have Wills

You may have seen a bumper sticker with the slogan "He who dies with the most toys wins!" A female version might read: "She who lives longest wins!" He may die with toys, but she'll get the last laugh when she inherits them all.

Women's longevity edge over men means that as part of our financial education we have to become knowledgeable about estate planning—the process of preparing a plan to administer and dispose of our property when we die. Not only are we increasingly earning our own incomes and acquiring assets in our own names, but our estate plans typically have more influence than those of our spouses in determining how family wealth is passed to subsequent generations. Because our spouses often predecease us, it is left to us to decide who inherits our assets and who can make decisions about them. We become perched in the proverbial catbird seat, left to determine the disposition of what will become family or shared wealth in ways that our husbands or partners might never have contemplated. As a result, our estate planning has to become more creative and, unfortunately, more complicated.

The fact that estate planning is complicated is probably one of the reasons most women avoid it. A Women and Company survey released in March 2006 found that while over 40 percent of women periodically review their financial situation, only 13 percent have executed a will, living will, and health care proxy. Women are becoming more comfortable about owning assets, but are not making decisions about how these assets should be dealt with when they die.

Part of the problem may be that estate planning is regarded as a stuffy and gloomy activity. The term conjures up visions of a dark oak-paneled room, presided over by a dour-faced attorney. One thinks of piles of documents, safety deposit boxes, and strategies for tax avoidance. The whole topic seems daunting, unfriendly, and, well, postponable. Worse still, estate planning forces you to confront your own death. It is often euphemistically referred to as "getting affairs in order," but this does little to hide the macabre overtones. Perhaps changing the term "estate planning" to a more user-friendly, positive expression, such as "getting organized," would go some way toward motivating women to plan their estates. Just about every woman I know likes to get organized, and lives and dies (pardon the pun) by her lists.

While most women may not have wills in the legal sense, they certainly have wills in the sense that they have intentions about what they want to do with their assets. So let us begin there as a way to start talking about estate planning. Putting the legal issues aside, if we approach of estate planning initially as a way to get organized about what should happen to your things should you no longer be there to manage them, we may succeed in getting more women to start the planning process.

WHERE THERE'S A WILL, THERE'S A WAY

All too often, people hire an attorney to execute their estate plan before they have properly considered their intentions. This can lead to serious and sometimes bizarre consequences. I had one client whose attorney talked him into establishing a qualified personal residence trust for tax-savings purposes. This meant, in effect, that he no longer owned his home outright, even though he was living there. A few years after establishing the trust he forgot that he no longer owned the home and, not once but twice, tried to transfer title to the home to someone else! Several hours of frantic phone calls and e-mails later he was wondering if all those tax savings were really worth it.

You have to know exactly what you have before you can decide what should be done with it.

A consideration of your intentions naturally has to start with an inventory of your assets. You may have thought that the asset inventory I asked you to create in Chapter 3 was just to prepare you for college savings or retirement. In fact, you were also doing advance work to plan for your estate. You have to know exactly what you have before you can decide what should be done with it.

Next, you have to talk to your intended beneficiaries, your family and friends, about what you want to have happen to your estate. Talking to your children about your vision for the family vacation property, for instance, or your hopes that they use their inheritances for the grandkids' education, is worth more than pages of complicated and formidable trust language. Furthermore, if they know "what Mom said she wanted," it may save them from slugging it out in court.

I sometimes think of estate planning as a field, with the person doing the planning at one end and her goals at the other. Between the two are many deep wells representing the contingencies, legalities, and special circumstances that are so easy to fall into along the way. It is important that you don't disappear down one such well or another, losing sight of what you want. This happens all too often when women go to an attorney without first seriously thinking about their wills (in the non-legal sense), and come away with trusts and documents they do not entirely understand.

EXERCISE 8–1. HOW DO YOU WANT TO MAKE THAT GIFT: WITH OR WITHOUT STRINGS?

Here's a way to keep estate planning simple, at least initially. Imagine you are in a room with everyone and everything you care about gathered around you. This includes your family and friends, and also charities. We will assume Uncle Sam is not invited, no matter how patriotic you are. Put on the table, metaphorically speaking, everything you have: your personal belongings, bank accounts, house, and pensions. Pick each item up and give it to whomever you wish. As you do, say: "I give this [name of possession] to you." Then pause to think about what you have done before you pick up the next item.

What came to mind during that pause? Maybe it was only a sense of benevolence and fulfilled intention. On the other hand, in making a particular gift, a "but" may have come into your mind, some condition or proviso you wanted to attach. Here are some of the more obvious:

- But I don't want your next wife to get it.
- But I don't want it going to your bill collectors.
- But make sure you use it to take care of your sister.
- But I want you to spend it on college or your first home.
- But only while you are alive.
- But not until you are old enough to handle it.
- But . . .

All those buts represent wells of complexity in the field of estate planning. Although I do not intend to take you down these wells, you need to know they are conditions an attorney will have to address.

There are, however, two buts that commonly arise during this exercise that you can address yourself. One is: "But it is not enough." This arises when you have insufficient assets in your estate to take care of your heirs or beneficiaries. If what you have on the table cannot take care of the needs of your survivors in the event of your death, you must purchase an amount of life insurance that will cover those needs at as little cost to you as possible. Fortunately, this is one of the simpler tasks in estate planning.

The other is: "But not now." This arises if you are afraid to make a gift because you are worried there will not be enough left for you. Although most assets in your estate usually pass to your beneficiaries after your death, in some cases it is recommended that you transfer some assets before death to obtain tax benefits—by putting assets into trust, for example, or recapitalizing your business and giving your children ownership shares. However, this involves giving up all or some of your control over your assets while you are still alive. If relinquishing this control comes at the expense of your peace of mind, no amount of tax savings will be worth it. Be sure to let your attorney know your thoughts on this issue.

NOT JUST THE WHAT BUT THE WHO OF ESTATE PLANNING

The giving exercise focuses on the things or assets in your estate—the house, car, and investments—and who will get them—your spouse, children, favorite charities, or friends. Anyone planning their estate should first spend a lot of time thinking about these issues. What is often not considered as carefully, but should be, is who will be responsible to make sure your wishes are carried out after your death or incapacity—the executors, guardians, and trustees, among others, who will manage and settle your estate. It is not unusual for us to find ourselves in the attorney's office and, when asked to name an executor or trustee, to grab the name of the nearest bank or attorney as the best person for the job.

You have to understand the roles of the various people who will manage your estate, what it takes to fulfill those roles, and what skills and attributes you should look for in suitable candidates.

To avoid this, you have to understand the roles of the various people who will manage your estate, what it takes to fulfill those roles, and what skills and attributes you should look for in suitable candidates. Remember that you are literally hiring these people for these tasks, even if you are not necessarily paying them. This means you need to talk to them first to determine whether they are even willing to do the job.

The following is a summary of some of the more common roles in the administration of an estate.

Guardian

If you are a mother or caretaker, naming someone to take care of your dependents in the event of your death is the most important—and often the most difficult—consideration. You must execute a will to designate a guardian. Many people think that without assets, there is no need for a will. But, in fact, even the Old Woman Who Lived in a Shoe, who had plenty of kids but little to give them, would have been wise to prepare a will, if only to name a guardian.

When considering a guardian for your child, you will want to name someone who shares your values and attitudes toward child rearing. Of course, no one will seem entirely adequate because, after all—who can replace you? But you will have to do the best you can. Naming a guardian is better than not having one at all, should the worst happen. Otherwise, the decision will be made by a possibly harried judge who does not even know you or your child.

You also have to consider the extra financial burden you will be asking your guardian to take on. If you plan to provide the child with money through life insurance or otherwise, think about whether the person you are considering as a guardian is financially responsible enough to handle this aspect. Look at how he or she handles money now. (Although I would never draw hard-and-fast conclusions about the negative correlation between kind-heartedness and financial savvy, I find it remarkable the number of times my clients have commented: "Oh, so and so would make a great mother, but she is a complete disaster with money.") If there is an inverse relationship between a person's ability to care for your child and their ability to manage money, you could name them as guardian of the child but name another person who is better with finances as a trustee of your child's money.

Executor/Executrix

This individual will carry out the terms of your will. She or he will be responsible for obtaining death certificates, arranging your funeral or memorial service, notifying creditors and account holders of your death, setting up your estate, filing any necessary information returns, and paying estate taxes. An executor is needed from the time of your death to the time of final distribution of your assets. This may take anywhere from a few months, should you have a very small or simple estate, to a year or two. (The executor's task is made much easier, of course, if you have your financial affairs in order.) Like a good physician, a good executor should be trying to work himself out of a job as soon as possible.

An executor has to be someone who knows you well. If your wishes are not explicitly spelled out—which is often the case when it comes to handling personal effects—your executor should understand you well enough to know what you would have wanted. Ideally, your executor should also know your beneficiaries and be able to work and communicate well with them. This can get tricky if you name a family member, because complicated family dynamics are often at work. Ask yourself whether the executor would have to referee likely disputes, or whether her duties would negatively affect her relationship with your beneficiaries.

I declined to be my sister's sole executrix because I have no interest in being the bad cop to a nephew who will undoubtedly be first in line for whatever cash would be available from the estate. My relationship with my nephew will continue to work if I remain his kind, caring, and uninvolved aunt, but not if I have to stand between him and what he may regard as the keys to a brand new car.

Where potentially problematic issues exist, there is always the option of naming a professional or corporate executor, usually a bank or trust company. There is no way my nephew will needle and charm a bank officer the way I know he can me. A trade-off is involved, of course: third-party objectivity will supplant any intimate knowledge of the deceased and the intended beneficiaries. You can also expect to pay more for an institutional or professional fiduciary. Another option is to name both an individual and a corporate executor to collaborate, or to allow an individual executor to hire a corporate entity for support should he require it.

Trustee

A trustee manages or administers a trust—property or other assets held for the benefit of another person. The duties of a trustee will be determined by terms set out in a governing trust agreement, or, alternatively, your will. The primary reason for creating a trust is to avoid an outright distribution of an asset or assets to your heirs. (Remember all the buts of the giving exercise you did before?) Instead, the benefit of the asset is doled out over time, sometimes in perpetuity.

Given the long-term nature of trusts, the trustee you choose needs to have some staying power.

Given the long-term nature of trusts, the trustee you choose needs to have some staying power. You might think twice, for instance, about naming your ninety-year-old father as a trustee. A trustee also needs to be financially savvy, since the role will be to ensure that the assets of the trust are managed appropriately and that the necessary annual filings are made to the IRS and the beneficiaries. A trustee needs to be aware of and empathetic to the needs and circumstances of the beneficiaries, but not subservient to them. The trustee's boss is the trust document, not the trust beneficiaries.

Many people opt for a bank or corporate trust company to be the trustee. The benefit is that these companies have objectivity, the necessary financial and tax expertise, and perpetual life (though the recent failures, consolidations, and mergers of financial companies may have you thinking otherwise). If you do name a bank or trust company, you may want to put a successors and assigns clause in your trust document so that if, say, Wachovia merges into Wells Fargo, your trust doesn't skip a beat.

Substitute decision-maker

Over the past thirty years, our life expectancy has increased significantly. But so, too, has the incidence of dementia or mental impairment in our final years. Accordingly, estate planning has expanded to include situations where you may be alive but incapable of making decisions about your finances or health care. The one positive outcome of the Terri Schiavo case—in which relatives of a Florida woman in a persistent vegetative state battled over whether or not a feeding tube should be removed—is that we are much more aware of the importance of planning for these contingencies.

The various agents you can name to make these types of decisions for you include:

- An attorney-in-fact
- An individual who holds a power of attorney, which becomes effective in the event of your disability or incapacity
- A health care agent, who can make medical decisions when you cannot
- An agent named in a living will or advanced directive, who can decide what measures are necessary or appropriate if you become terminally ill

In appointing a guardian, executor, trustee, or substitute decision-maker, you will also want to name a successor in case your original designee declines or is unable, for whatever reason, to carry out the necessary duties. You will also want to ensure that the people you choose can hire the help they need to carry out their responsibilities. Finally, consider the possibility of paying any individuals you choose. (Corporate entities always get paid, of course.)

In the case of an executor, if the individual is also a beneficiary it may be more advantageous to provide them with a larger gift out of the estate than to pay them a fee. The reason is that a fee is considered taxable income, while a distribution may not be taxable or may be taxed at a lower rate. With respect to a trustee, it is more customary to remunerate them based on a percentage of the assets being administered.

ONE SIZE DOESN'T FIT ALL WOMEN

Most estate planning advice out there is geared to the average adult: a person married once who intends to stay that way, with children, concerned about the taxability of the estate, and highly averse to probate—often without really understanding what probate is. But women's estate needs and issues don't always come in average sizes. We may have remained single by choice or we may have divorced. We may not have family members around who know our intentions should we be rendered mentally or physically incapable. Believe it or not, we may not even care about taxes if children or close family are not in the picture. Here, therefore, is some less traditional advice.

Lifetime giving

Assets transferred to an American spouse are not taxed during life or at death. This marital exemption does not, therefore, benefit a single woman or a female with a same-sex partner or non-American spouse. If you fall into this category, you do have a personal exemption whereby up to $3.5 million in assets can be transferred at death without incurring federal estate tax. (Note: this is the exemption amount for deaths occurring in 2009; this amount will certainly be changing in the future as Congress again takes up the debate about estate taxation.)

Beyond the personal exemption, if you wish to minimize taxes and do not have a regulation-sized husband to give assets to tax-free, you should consider taking aggressive advantage of the standard gift tax exemption by giving up to $13,000 per year tax-free to your partner or other beneficiary. (More can be given to a non-U.S. spouse under the same principle of an annual gift exempt from taxes.) In other words, if you have considerable wealth but no American or heterosexual spouse, you may wish to shift your estate planning emphasis from testamentary giving (i.e., giving at death) to lifetime giving.

Charitable giving

If you do not have immediate family, or what the estate planning profession likes to call "natural objects of your bounty," giving to charity may become central to your estate planning. Remember to be strategic and thoughtful. Your charitable gifts become the children you leave behind. What a family trust may be to a mother, a foundation may be to you. It becomes your way of creating the lasting legacy of what you valued most in life.

Circling In on Charitable Giving

Philanthropy does not have to be a solitary activity for rich old ladies. Join with other women to create a giving circle. Dues are collected to fund gifts to charitable organizations that the circle is interested in and has researched. One such giving circle was formed as a supper club, where everyone contributed the cost of an average family dinner and the proceeds were donated to organizations dedicated to helping the hungry.

Hen planning

When it comes to leaving everything to a spouse, our first thought is often: "What happens if he gets married again?" followed by: "Where would that leave my kids?" These ruminations can take us from being as mad as a wet hen to being as protective as a mother hen. Wives need to plan for these contingencies by means of appropriate trusts as advised by an attorney, even when it may seem unloving to do so. We have mentioned the statistical likelihood of women surviving their husbands. But another compelling statistic is that men are much more likely to remarry after losing their wives than vice versa. Recent studies have found that the average replacement time for lost wives is a mere two and a half years. Therefore, we need to plan unsentimentally and realistically for this possibility by making sure that what is ours remains so, even after we're gone.

The biggest fear most women have is that they may become a bag lady.

Planned giving or split gifts

The biggest fear most women have is that they may become a bag lady. They are afraid of getting old, running out of money, and having no one to take care of them. They don't like to think about giving during their lifetime, or setting up estate planning mechanisms for tax benefits that cede control of assets while they are alive. For these women, who may still have generous hearts, the solution when it comes to their children or charities is planned or split-interest giving. This entails setting up remainder trusts or annuities, personal or charitable, that transfer assets to beneficiaries in a tax-advantaged way while providing a lifetime or term income from those assets to the donor. A personal residence trust works in a similar way. The donor might effectively give a home or vacation property to her children, but retain the right to live there for a specified time. Such "mine now, yours later" planning has tremendous appeal for women who want to give, but without losing control.

MAKE IT LEGAL

Once you have considered what your estate will consist of and who will get and manage it, you will need the assistance of an attorney to help you execute your estate plan. One reason is that, although your intentions may be relatively simple, the execution can quickly become complex. Much of the blame lies with our highly convoluted system of gift and estate taxation. Potential tax consequences of a gift or bequest to both the donor and recipient are dependent upon the amount of the gift, the relationship between the donor and recipient, and the timing of the gift. If clients call me asking whether it would be okay to send their grandchild a check for college tuition, for example, I cannot give them a simple, unqualified yes or no answer. Instead, I must preface my answer with a lengthy discussion of the relevant tax legislation governing the treatment of such gifts.

Even if gift and estate taxes did not exist—as is perennially proposed and rejected during every legislative cycle—estate planning would still be complicated as a result of our complex lives. Divorce, multiple marriages, blended families, non-traditional domestic partnerships, special needs, and family dysfunction—all these modern-day realities conspire to make it more difficult to transfer assets in a direct or straightforward way. It is ironic, perhaps, that the one area of personal financial management that should come so easily to women—giving—is so fraught with constraints and conditions.

You also need legal expertise to help you with the proper titling of your assets; the drafting of your will, powers of attorney, and medical directives; and the establishment of trusts or other entities. But while an attorney will assist you with the legalities, you must keep your focus on how your estate plan will carry out your intentions.

I offer the following pointers for your consideration in dealing with your attorney to execute your estate plan. (By the way, I often accompany my clients to the attorney's office to provide the financial context for the estate plan. Serving simultaneously as advocate and interpreter is a great role for your financial planner.)

Make your attorney accountable

Don't be intimidated by topics you don't fully understand by not asking questions, afraid you will look dumb. Keep your attorney accountable by asking—repeatedly if necessary—what her or his strategy entails, what purposes it serves, and what the downsides or disadvantages might be. In my annual meetings with my clients, we revisit the terms of their estate plan—what they are and why they are included—since it is not at all unusual for the clients to forget these details.

Implement your plan

Your attorney will ask you to do certain things to carry out your plan: retitle this asset, fund that trust, change this beneficiary designation. Telling you to do these things is not equivalent to getting them done. If failing to plan is the number one mistake women make, failing to put the plan into effect is number one-and-a-half.

Stay in the present

Remember that you are making your plan so that if you died today your estate could be settled easily and efficiently. Do not worry about every future contingency that may result in changes in your assets or beneficiaries. There is a certain amount of standard contingency planning that your attorney will have you do, but don't try to address every possibility.

Review and revise your plan as necessary

Once your estate plan is complete, each time you open a new account or purchase a new major asset, ask yourself where the asset should go in the event of your death and whether the titling on the new asset accomplishes this. Furthermore, any time there is a major change with respect to your assets, your beneficiaries, or your state of residence, check in with your planner or attorney to discuss the impact on your plan.

There is a saying that goes, "Never let the perfect become the enemy of the good." This is probably more applicable to estate planning than to any other area of personal financial management. If you find that the decisions you have to make are difficult, take heart: they're not easy for anyone. But don't let their difficulty prevent you from making them. Accept that there can never be enough specificity in a written document to make sure your family and friends get exactly what they need and not what they don't. Some written instructions are better than none at all. Accept that there can never be a perfect person to do the work of your life—raise your children, provide for your friends and family, support your causes—but there are some capable choices. The best we can do is to try to make good decisions, which is to say, well-considered ones.

SUGGESTED ROUTES

www.caringinfo.org
This is the website for Caring Connections, a consumer education program run by the National Hospice and Palliative Care Organization to help individuals dealing with end-of-life issues. Caring Connections provides information on advance directives and state-specific forms which can be downloaded.

Calligaro, Julie A. *Arranging Your Financial and Legal Affairs: A Step-By-Step Guide to Getting Your Affairs in Order*, Women's Source Books, 1998.

Whitman, Wynne A. *Smart Women Protect Their Assets: Essential Information for Every Woman About Wills, Trusts, and More*, FT Press, 2009.

Chapter Nine

Women Inspire

I have always considered my job as a financial planner to be three parts educator and one part advisor. I tell people what to do with their money, but not without first making sure that they understand how money works. My female clients are especially interested in the education aspect. As one told me when she hired me: "I want the bottom line, but only after you explain to me how you get there."

Getting financially educated is important to most women, but even more important is their wish for their children to get this education. Over the years I have held and attended seminars on raising fiscally responsible children. I recall one such program entitled "The Giving Child," which focused on helping children learn generosity and social awareness in a world of consumerism and instant gratification. After discussing how to encourage children to share and even give, we turned to the more difficult issue of how parents can share their financial experiences with their children. I say "difficult" because most parents are uncomfortable talking about finances, especially their own finances, with their offspring. One woman confidently stood up. "It's very simple," she said. "When my son comes to me and asks, 'Are we rich, Mommy?' I tell him, 'Daddy and I are. But you are not.' "

Most people would envy her directness. For the majority of us, teaching children about money is like teaching them about sex. We find it a very awkward, personal topic to broach. While we want to help our children find their own financial way, we are embarrassed to discuss the subject for fear of revealing our own financial status or spending practices.

As with the issue of sex, however, it is crucial that we engage in a discussion about money with our children. Like it or not, we are the source of most of their beliefs and attitudes about money. Unless we teach them the good—as well as the bad and the ugly—about the subject, they will grow up with the popular misconception that making, managing, and spending it is easy. In our culture, money, like sex, is often perceived as abundant and readily available. Parents are devoted to providing their children with good educations—which lead to good jobs and good incomes—but less often have given thought to the financial education their children desperately need to handle the money once they earn it. Our schools, meanwhile, have done a miserable job teaching money management skills as part of their curriculum. At most, kids are exposed to a few dollars-and-cents problems in their math classes.

The result is financially illiterate young adults who have no tangible sense of how to deal with the variety of issues inherent in managing money. Failed by society, schools, and parents, many are poorly equipped to grasp even the basics. They are confused about the tax liabilities on their earnings, the true cost of living, the implications of debt, the benefits of deferred gratification, how to save, or how to invest money. They believe that savings means getting 50 percent off and that responsible money management is making minimum payments on their credit cards or transferring balances to lower-interest lenders.

TEACH YOUR CHILDREN WELL

To improve this state of affairs, we have to start by increasing our own financial know-how and translating that into healthy financial habits. It is my hope that the discussion in this book is a move in that direction. Next, we have to impart these skills to our children.

Let's begin by trying to define what success would look like. What do you hope for your child when it comes to financial responsibility? The following are some frequent responses I receive from clients:

- I want my child to respect money, but not be ruled by it.
- I want my child to learn to be generous.
- I want my child to be prudent in using debt.
- I want my child to stand on her or his own financially.
- I want my child to be free of financial worries, able to provide for her own needs and those of her family.

Thinking as carefully as you can about what financial responsibility would look like in your child is the first step to developing the lessons you hope to teach.

Your own list may be more specific—"I want my child to get a place of his own" or "I want my child to start paying for her own car expenses"—but the point is the same. Thinking as carefully as you can about what financial responsibility would look like in your child is the first step to developing the lessons you hope to teach. These lessons should then be imparted by example, practical advice, and, yes, even some formal study.

First and foremost, your kids are watching you, perhaps more closely than you think. How you handle money, how you talk about it, and what emotions you express with respect to it are all inputs to your children's eventual understanding and attitude toward their finances. Many of you might be surprised at what children take away from their observations.

I remember at the age of about four watching my parents play Monopoly and deducing from their actions and conversation that the paper bills they were passing back and forth had extraordinary power. Apparently, you could use these slips of paper to get what you wanted, like houses or passes out of jail. I waited until they left their Monopoly game and slipped a few $100 bills into my pocket. The next day, I toddled into the candy store, confident that all the penny candy behind the glass counter would be mine. Unfortunately, the hard-hearted storekeeper thought otherwise.

It may take time, effort, and some creativity, but there are many opportunities to transform what you consider routine money transactions into lessons to teach your kids. Women are responsible for as much as 80 percent of their households' financial transactions. In any given day there are at least half a dozen teachable moments in which we could begin to take some of the mystery out of money for our children.

Consider, for instance, taking your child inside the bank instead of using the ATM. Talk to your child about the role of banks as places where we hold our money for safekeeping and (theoretically) growth. For an older child, explain why you prefer your chosen bank over another. Does it provide more interest, lower fees, or more convenience? Talk about the amount of money you are depositing or withdrawing, where the deposit came from, and where and how you plan to use the funds withdrawn.

Get them to help you pay the bills. A friend of mine who hated to pay bills always got out a jug of wine and a pack of cigarettes when it was time to write the checks. She wonders why her daughter, now an adult with a well-paying job, has trouble with creditors. Consider making the task of bill paying a pleasant, or even fun, occasion for your kids. By all means, make it a regular event. If your kids can read, have them open the bills, identify what they are for, and circle the amounts payable and the due dates. This should give them an appreciation for routine living expenses.

They may not realize, for example, that we pay for things like water or condo fees. Show them what is involved in writing out a check or entering a bill payment online. An appalling number of children leave home with no idea how to maintain a check register. As a result, they keep overdrawing their accounts because they rely on what the ATM tells them they have available.

Have your children help prepare a shopping list and check things off in the store. Talk out loud as you comparison shop—explain why you believe this item is a better buy than that one. Introduce them to the concept of unit costs, which are posted in most grocery stores, and how this information impacts your buying decisions. Explain to them why brand items are more expensive than generic. Help them understand where coupons can help save money and when they can cause you to spend more money.

What's important is to engage your children so they appreciate the limitations and responsibilities, as well as the benefits, involved in dealing with money.

The list of daily financial events worth talking about to your kids is much longer, of course: budgeting, tipping, making money arrangements for a trip, and so on. What's important is to engage your children so they appreciate the limitations and responsibilities, as well as the benefits, involved in dealing with money.

You will likely find that by being accountable to your children about your financial choices, you yourself will become more financially responsible. Telling your kids to stand tall will have you standing taller. Just try, for example, explaining to your child your rationale the next time you stop to pick up a lottery ticket. My guess is that you won't buy the ticket.

You might also consider directing your older children to resources that discuss higher-level financial concepts, such as markets, investment, or retirement planning.

In this increasingly sophisticated world, it is important that our kids are at least familiar with these concepts, which they will have to grapple with as adults. Fortunately, this is also an age of proliferating information that your children can take advantage of. The U.S. government, in particular, is making efforts to disseminate information to improve this country's level of financial competence. In 2003, the U.S. Financial Literacy and Education Commission was established to coordinate the educational materials and outreach efforts of all the federal agencies that deal with financial matters and markets. These materials can be conveniently accessed at www.mymoney.gov. Another leader in this area is the National Endowment for Financial Education (NEFE) (www.nefe.org). PTA-active moms interested in getting a financial literacy program going at their children's school can contact NEFE's High School Financial Planning Program to obtain free materials (http://hsfpp.nefe.org/home/).

BEGIN WITH THE BASICS

As a prerequisite to financial maturity, our children must understand a number of concepts, including the power of compound interest, the importance of diversification, the difference between real and nominal returns, the reasons for and the financial impact of inflation, the effect of taxes on earnings and savings, and the difference between investing as an owner of a company (i.e., a stockholder) and a lender to a company (i.e., a bondholder).

But if I had only one hour to talk to a preteen or teenager to help her make her way in the financial world, I would focus on two basic principles that form the underpinnings of most financial decisions she will have to make. These concepts are critical to, but often missing from, people's understanding of finance.

The first is opportunity cost. This is the idea that everything we buy, every asset we acquire, and every financial benefit we choose has a cost—not only in terms of dollars, but in terms of forgone opportunity. Opportunity costs are all the other choices not made. The second concept is the risk/return trade-off associated with any investment; returns we seek from our financial activities always have commensurate risks.

Both the opportunity cost principle and the principle of risk/return trade-off are principles of balance—itself a fundamental accounting principle. Kids (and adults who have not attained financial maturity) tend to be unaware of them and, therefore, view assets or investments one-dimensionally. They will think about what they can get (the upside of buying or investing), but not what they may give up or risk in the process (the downside).

You can begin to inspire an understanding of these principles in your child by emphasizing that there is an upside and a downside to every financial choice. The next time she receives $50 from Grandma, for instance, and wants to go straight to RadioShack to get whatever gadget is priced at $50, ask her to consider what she won't be able to do if she chooses to spend her money this way. Or when your child decides that all he wants is to be a professional football player or a rap star because of the allure of a seven-figure income, encourage him to think about the risks associated with such careers.

These lessons can be taken overboard, of course. I have seen adults paralyzed by the existence of alternatives when it comes to making a financial decision. Dwelling on risk can also keep investors frozen and indecisive. The last thing we want to do is hamstring our kids' financial judgment by asking them to overthink their choices. Nevertheless, I believe that taking the time to introduce your child to the merits of weighing benefits against associated costs or risks is time well spent.

ENCOURAGE LEARNING BY DOING

Along the way to good money management, children must get their own hands-on experience. The two most common vehicles are an allowance and money gifts—and I am convinced there are right and wrong ways to give both.

Let's start with allowances. The debate about whether kids should earn an allowance is longstanding: one side claims that children should not be paid to contribute to the household. Everyone needs to do their part, goes the argument, whether or not they get paid. The other camp says that allowances provide children with their first experience of merit pay. As a business owner, I experienced a similar debate with respect to bonus payments: should employees get a bonus for doing a great job at what is expected of them?

But I don't believe the issue as to whether an allowance is earned or given is nearly as important as the issue of how an allowance is used. Kids need to learn from an early age that there are numerous and competing claims on money: it can be spent, given away, saved, or invested. Their natural inclination, of course, is to spend money they get as soon as they get it. What they need to be taught is to divide their allowance (however they get it) into portions and to allocate various portions for specific purposes. They need to learn that instant gratification is not the only game in town, and that money must also be directed to other longer-term goals, such as saving to buy that more expensive item.

One of the biggest threats to our financial security as adults is living from paycheck to paycheck—or worse, paycheck to line of credit. Children allowed to spend whatever they get as soon as they get it learn this bad habit, which is likely to carry over into adulthood.

One of the biggest threats to our financial security as adults is living from paycheck to paycheck—or worse, paycheck to line of credit. Children allowed to spend whatever they get as soon as they get it learn this bad habit, which is likely to carry over into adulthood. If as children we all learned that a part of each paycheck is needed to last longer than a single pay period—because the supply of money does not always meet the demand for money—the financial woes we currently face as a country might be less severe.

For this reason, I consider the current popularity of gift cards detrimental to the financial education of our kids. I am pretty much alone in this view—kids love them and would rather get a gift card than have an adult choose a book or article of clothing. Adults like giving them—primarily to children—because they are convenient, are appreciated, and seem less crass than money. But in so doing, we rob our children of choice. When a child gets a $20 gift card from Banana Republic, his mission becomes finding and purchasing $20 worth of Banana Republic merchandise. If he buys less, he may lose some of the value of the card. This, in turn, usually induces him to buy more than the card is worth and spend more of his own money. The stores, meanwhile, are making profits from unused balances and additional expenditures. It would be far better to give the child a $20 bill and thereby open up the decision-making process of how and where to spend it, save it, or invest it. (Maybe you should suggest that your child buy stock in those stores that most aggressively market gift cards, as they will likely be profitable!)

I understand, of course, that the societal, commercial, and cultural influences on your child will be strong and that any sound financial lessons you try to impart will often go unheeded. If you find yourself still losing the battle by the time your child is a teenager, I have one more, somewhat unorthodox, suggestion: send her to a financial professional for an hour or two of counsel.

CAN YOU RELATE?

Being exemplary role models to our children is crucial. But you should also be aware of the limitations. On several occasions, clients have come to me perplexed as to why one of their children is a total spendthrift while the other cannot let go of a dollar without an audible cry of pain. Both kids had the same household experience around money, so why did they turn out so differently? To my knowledge, there is no credible behavioral research on this issue. My own theory is that siblings, and even husbands and wives, sometimes develop opposite attitudes about money as a way to avoid being overwhelmed or engulfed by the other's style. She spends because he saves. You plan because I don't. He holds onto money because his brother always needs bailing out. Being aware of these patterns is a first step to addressing them.

It may surprise you to know that I learned this suggestion from my clients rather than the other way around. They would occasionally ask me if I would be willing to meet with their children, usually before they went away to college or if they were about to receive a significant sum of money from a trust or inheritance. Over time, I began to suggest this to other clients with teenage kids because I could see what a positive effect it had. The teens would initially sit slouched in my conference room, but eventually they sat up straighter, encouraged by being treated as adults even if their financial knowledge was extremely elementary. The benefit was not necessarily that they learned a great deal about money management. It was that they began to regard themselves as independent financial decision-makers who could use money to shape their future, provided they took seriously the responsibility of managing it. What is the key to the success of these meetings? You, the parent, should not be in the room.

Circling In on Family Finance

Next time there is a big family party or a trip in the offing, get everyone together to discuss not just the logistics of time, place, and who is bringing what, but the financial implications of the event. Talk about a budget and ideas for keeping costs in line. Consider giving each member of the family a line item in the budget to manage; for example, give your ten-year-old a dollar amount he can spend on decorations, and your teenager the financial and creative discretion to put together the music.

Motherhood presents a dilemma: we want to protect our offspring while encouraging them to be independent. I began this chapter with the story of the woman who told her child bluntly that her financial circumstances were not his. This may be a healthy approach, but how realistic is it? After all, most parents want to make their children's lives better than their own. The inevitable result is that on numerous occasions we give or lend our children our money.

There are no rules for how much money or support you should give or not give your children. Generosity can be as crushing as stinginess, just as saying no can be as liberating as largesse. What is important is that we talk about these issues with our children. It can even mean committing, where applicable, our discussions to writing—developing a loan document when lending money, for instance, or, for multigenerational wealth transfers, creating a narrative of your family's wealth, how it was created, and what it meant, to pass along to your children.

CAN YOU RELATE?

Our conversations with our children are full of gender stereotypes, many unconscious. "When a girl babysits, grown-ups praise her for how well she deals with children. But when a boy mows neighbors' lawns, no one says he's good with lawns; they say he's a budding businessman."—"Women and Financial Empowerment: Why Women are Statistically Behind the Eight Ball," Lili A. Vasileff, published in Garden State Woman magazine's annual Financial Resources Guide, 2005.

Based on my two-plus decades of practice, I can say unequivocally that the biggest failure with respect to raising financially responsible kids is neglecting to communicate to them our intentions, expectations, and hopes when it comes to money. We must provide our children with solid financial directions if we want them to handle their money at least as well as, and possibly better than, we do ourselves. The financial health of the next generation starts with us.

For the sake of our children and ourselves, we need to work to change our own perceptions that financial issues are too layered and too esoteric for us to tackle. They are not. As discussed earlier, our financial decisions reflect our very values and are the means to realize our hopes and dreams. What could be more important? It's my hope that this book has provided you with a road map and started you in the right direction.

It's a question of women's worth. Your worth.

SUGGESTED ROUTES

www.dianachambers.com
Diana Chambers, founder of The Chambers Group, is a family wealth consultant who specializes in communication among family members about money. Available on the website (under Resource Material) is an article written by Diana Chambers titled "Children & Money: How Can We Guide Them?"

www.mymoney.gov
Established by the U.S. Financial Literacy and Education Commission, this website is a comprehensive government clearinghouse of financial education, literacy programs, and tools offered through various government agencies.

www.nefe.org
The website for the private, not-for-profit National Endowment for Financial Education. Provides financial literacy tools and materials, as well as information on partnering efforts with other organizations committed to the financial education of Americans.

www.virginmoneyus.com
Virgin Money offers a management program for loans between family members or friends, which puts such loans on a formal, and thereby more successful, footing through the use of loan documentation, terms, oversight, and reporting.

Schwab-Pomeranz, Carrie, and Charles Schwab. *It Pays to Talk: How to Have the Essential Conversations with Your Family about Money and Investing*, Crown Publishing Group, 2003.

Women's Words

A Female-Friendly Glossary of Financial Terms

Sometimes our journey toward financial enlightenment is suspended or halted for the simple reason that it involves too many words that are foreign to us.

It is one thing to know what a technical term or phrase means; it is quite another to understand it and weave it into our experience. For the first kind of knowledge, I direct my women readers to Investopedia (www.investopedia.com), a website for financial education, which has an online dictionary of more than 7,000 terms. You can also sign up for a financial-word-of-the-day to be e-mailed to you.

Understanding is harder to come by. I have found that stories, analogies, even humor are often the most effective forms of explanation, and that these speak to the creative, intuitive side of women's brains, where real wisdom resides.

Accordingly, I leave financial definitions to the writers of dictionaries or textbooks and offer instead the following less conventional explanations for some of the financial terms used in this book.

Advance directive: Just-in-case instructions that are every bit as important as the list of emergency numbers you leave on your refrigerator or the notes you give to the babysitter. In the case of an advance directive, the instructions pertain to your wishes about your medical treatment at the end of your life and your choice of who will make medical decisions for you if you cannot.

Alternative Minimum Tax (AMT): Like trouble and debt, AMT is something you get into often without knowing it. There is nothing *minimum* about AMT, since it refers to a computation of your tax liability using a method different from that on your 1040 form, and if the taxes thereby computed are higher than what is on your regular tax return, you must pay the greater amount. Originally intended by Congress to prevent wealthy taxpayers from using deductions and exemptions to whittle away their tax liability to almost nothing, the AMT no longer serves its social policy purpose. Again, as with debt, far too many people are in it who should not be. The AMT will soon be fixed, it is hoped. Until then, do not do your taxes yourself without an up-to-date software program that will run the AMT computation in the background and tell you if you are in it. Not knowing does not cut it with the IRS.

Annuity: If life is a gamble, similar to "heads I live" and "tails I die," then buying an annuity is a way to hedge against the first outcome, while buying life insurance is a way to hedge against the second. An annuity is a guarantee, issued by a life insurance company, to pay you a stipulated amount monthly, quarterly, or yearly for as long as you live. Thus it serves the simple purpose of providing you an income, usually in retirement, that you cannot outlive. What you really need to know about annuities, however, is that they are almost never sold or used for this very simple purpose, but rather (like their cousin, life insurance) are promoted for all sorts of other reasons: as tax savings, hedges against stock market risk, and a tax-free source of funds. Do not be distracted when it comes to buying an annuity. Keep costs low and quality of guarantee high.

Asset: Anything that you and at least one other reasonable person agree has a monetary value. It's important to have this third-party concurrence, since without it your asset cannot be exchanged or sold for something else you need or want. Thus, your skills and experience are assets if an employer is willing to pay for them (see Chapter 4, "Women Work—Maximizing Your Human Capital"); your trenchant sense of humor is probably not.

Asset allocation: The art and science of making good investment pies. Every asset class (ingredient) must be measured, and must enhance the return or lower the risk (think of them as flavors), but it is the overall performance (taste) that must meet the investor's risk tolerance (palate).

Asset location: Not only do we have to choose our asset classes when making investment pies, we also have to decide which pie to put them into. We make the distinction between pies that are taxable and pies that are tax-deferred or nontaxable. A basic rule that financial experts and pundits love to debate, but which nevertheless holds stubbornly true, is as follows: emphasize high-growth assets in your tax-deferred accounts (i.e., IRAs, 401(k)s) and low-growth assets in your taxable account.

Behavioral finance: The field of market economics that studies neither the bulls nor the bears, but the herd of cows that follows them without really knowing why. Behavioral finance focuses on the non-rational way we make financial decisions—on our extreme aversion to loss, for example, or our inflated sense of having above-average decision-making capabilities.

Bond: A bond is usually contrasted with a stock as one of the two major forms of investment. To understand the difference, consider the following parable. A man in a small village sets up a business making soup. To get started, he needs bowls. A woman comes to his shop with a bowl for the soup maker to use, but asks that the bowl be returned to her in a year's time. She also asks for a sample of soup each week until the time that the bowl must be returned. A second woman comes to the soup maker, and she too offers a bowl. In this case, however, she does not ask for the bowl back. Instead, she asks that if there is soup left over at the end of the day, she be allowed to sit down and eat with the soup maker. The first woman is essentially a bondholder: she lends her bowl (or capital) in return for a promise that her capital will be returned. The second woman is a stockholder: she asks for no guarantees, but instead believes that the soup maker will be successful enough to share his profits with her.

CERTIFIED FINANCIAL PLANNER™: Professionals who hold the CFP® designation are qualified by examination, experience, ongoing education, and compliance with an ethical code to advise individuals on matters of personal finance. I am a CFP® professional and proud of it.

Credit Shelter Trust: A classic example of the tax tail wagging the dog, a CST refers to money set aside in a given individual's estate and placed in a trust. The amount set aside is equal to the amount that IRS rules allow an individual to pass to any beneficiary estate-tax-free. The reason CSTs are more like wagging tails and less like whole dogs is that they are usually set up only for tax-saving purposes, and not necessarily because an individual would choose to direct money to his beneficiaries via this kind of trust or in the credit-equivalent amount.

Defined benefit plan: A type of retirement plan where what matters is the amount of money you get each month or year, not where the money is invested or how much there is. These are concerns only of the plan sponsors—a company or government—and not of the sponsor's retired employees. Sound almost too good to be true? They probably are, given that defined benefit plans are rapidly disappearing because plan sponsors are finding them too costly to maintain.

Defined contribution plan: In contrast to a defined benefit plan, a defined contribution retirement plan is one where the participant has to worry about how much goes into the plan and how it is invested. The most prevalent form of defined contribution plans are 401(k) plans. Given the lack of investing knowledge of the average plan participant and the recent meltdown of both stock and bond markets, many claim that 401(k) plans have been a colossal public policy mistake and have not provided adequately for Americans' retirement.

Equity: Often considered just a fancy synonym for stock, equity is, however, a broader concept, since we can have equity or ownership in assets or enterprises that do not issue stock. Think of your home, for example. Your home equity is your share of the home's value minus whatever funds you have borrowed to purchase or improve the home.

Estate taxes: The most important thing to understand about estate taxes is that they are separate and different from income taxes. So often people talk about all those taxes that have to be paid when someone dies, without realizing that there are two sorts: taxes that are assessed on income earned from the decedent's assets starting in the year in which the person died until the time that those assets are completely transferred to his beneficiaries, and estate taxes assessed on the net value of assets above a certain exemption amount. Ironically, the phrase "There is nothing certain but death and taxes" is not correct when it comes to estate taxes, since only a small percentage of wealthy individuals have to pay them. Income taxes are another matter.

Exchange-traded funds (ETFs): The financial world loves to take good ideas and try to make them better, or more confusing. Such is the case with ETFs. They are based on exactly the same principle as index mutual funds (see below), in that they are a basket of securities assembled to replicate the performance of a given market. The kicker in the case of ETFs is that, unlike mutual funds, they can be traded on an exchange any time of day. They can be bought and sold just like stocks. You can, for example, put in an order to buy an ETF only at a given price, or sell an ETF if it trades below a certain price. In essence, ETFs take a passive approach to investing (indexing) and make it available to active market traders. While I recommend ETFs for their low costs and diversification, they have been overmarketed as an investment that can be all things to all people.

Executor/Executrix: Also called a personal representative, this person makes sure that the provisions of your will are honored. Don't be put off by the grim formality of the term. This person should generally be a comfortable close friend or intimate other who knows what you would want, even if you haven't made it absolutely clear in your estate plan.

529 plan: Here's a hint: whenever you hear numbers in a financial term, it means that the product or strategy is governed by a tax statute and is, therefore, complicated and technical. (Other examples include 401(k) plan and 501(c)(3) organization.) A 529 plan is a gift you can make, usually to your child and always for post-secondary education, with tax strings attached. For the benefit of tax-free growth in the account, you have to abide by certain IRS provisions, such as using the money only for certain approved education costs. Sponsored by individual states, 529 plans are available through brokers and financial service providers. Shopping for one is a little like buying a car. There are so many different makes and models that it is easy to forget the real purpose for getting one: to get you or your child where you want to go, safely.

Fixed income: This is a generic term for the asset class of which bonds are a major part. Women like this asset class because of the fixed component, which sounds like a guarantee, and the income component, which they generally have unrealistic fears of losing or not having enough of. Most women need to learn to like fixed income less and equity investment more to be adequately prepared for retirement.

Guardian: If you are a parent or caretaker of a dependent, guardianship is possibly the most important role to be designated in your will. A guardian is needed for individuals who have not yet reached the age of financial majority (eighteen or twenty-one years, depending on the state of residence) or who are physically and/or mentally handicapped. But deciding on a guardian is also one of the most difficult choices to make. In essence, a guardian becomes your replacement as a caretaker, and there is simply no one in the world as well-qualified for this job as you. To make matters worse, husbands and wives almost never agree on who the guardian should be. You need to swallow hard and make this decision anyway.

Human capital: The sum total of your education, experience, and expertise as it commands value in the workplace. Unlike financial capital or real property, it can rarely be used as collateral for a loan or be borrowed against, but it is nevertheless likely to be your greatest asset in producing future wealth.

Index mutual funds: These can be thought of as market mirrors. These pools of securities have no investment strategy or identity of their own, nor are they managed by individuals who make deliberate, conscious choices of what to buy and sell in the fund. Their purpose is to hold up a mirror to a given investment market, such as the S&P 500 or the Morgan Stanley Europe, Asia, and Far East market, and to replicate the holdings and performance of these markets. Because they are not managed, except by a computer, index funds are generally very low-expense options for investors who want broad market diversification.

Liability: To put a positive spin on a balance sheet word generally understood as a negative, a liability can be thought of as a source of funds used to acquire an asset. Hence, we take out a car loan (liability) to acquire a car (asset), or a mortgage to acquire a home. When we see liabilities as such, it becomes a lot easier to understand the appropriate management of our debt: you want to make sure that the liability or funds borrowed decreases in value over time, while the asset thereby acquired grows in value. If only we had kept it that simple, the huge credit crisis of 2008–09 might never have happened.

Long-term care insurance: LTC insurance provides income in the event that you are unable to carry out normal daily activities on your own. My friend and associate Christine Fahlund of T. Rowe Price calls it "stay in your own home insurance." Another friend and colleague, the nationally known financial advisor Harold Evensky, defines it as disability income insurance for retirees. In so defining this term, he also reveals his opinion that it is as necessary for retirees as disability insurance is for working people.

To Harold's emphasis, I will add some urgency of my own. If you have visited any nursing homes lately, you are no doubt aware that the vast majority of residents are women.

Market efficiency: The story is told of two economics professors walking down a busy street. One sees a $20 on the sidewalk and bends down to pick it up. The other tells him not to bother because the bill must be an illusion. "If it were real," he explains, "it would not be left on the sidewalk." What the second professor is referring to is the efficient market, where information is instantly available to everyone. There are no extraordinary opportunities (i.e., stray $20 bills), because as soon as such opportunities appear, someone takes advantage of them and they disappear. The point here is that in a highly competitive market, such as the market for traded securities, it is a waste of time looking for $20 bills or the next hot stock.

Money: Grease, just grease. It does nothing on its own, but if applied consistently and carefully, it makes things run.

Mutual funds: Compared to a single security (bond or stock), a mutual fund is a pool or basket of securities chosen by a computer program or an investment manager to offer a diversified investment strategy. The irony of mutual funds is that there are more such baskets than there are security eggs (individual stocks and bonds) to put in them. This should be instructive to the average individual; marketing and packaging is just as powerful in the investment world as it is in the grocery store. If you want to buy a low-cost generic brand, go for an index fund or an ETF.

Non-qualified plan: This sounds like something you don't want as part of your investment portfolio, but in fact you do. The *non-qualified* descriptor simply explains its tax status and means that any income or gains of the plan or account are currently taxable. This is in contrast to retirement plans that are qualified by the IRS to defer taxes until the money is withdrawn. You want non-qualified plans, known more familiarly as brokerage accounts, as part of your investment holdings because these give you a choice when you need money in retirement: you can withdraw from your non-qualified account and not pay taxes, or withdraw from your 401(k) or IRA and pay the taxes that have been deferred. Having the flexibility to plan your taxes is important, as is saving more for your retirement by using both types of plans.

Power of attorney: A document that delegates decision-making authority to another individual, a power of attorney can ensure that what you want to happen with your assets or your health care will happen, even if you are not in a state to make decisions. It can be invoked if you are out of the country or if you are in a coma. Either way, it is important that you have prepared for such states by giving a power of attorney to a trusted friend or family member.

Qualified plan: The quality of being qualified comes from the IRS. Such a plan is governed under special tax provisions that allow the plan to grow without being taxed until the money is taken out.

Stock: See the parable of the soup maker under the definition for "Bond." There is an unfortunate tendency, which flourishes in bull markets, to think of stocks as having value unto themselves without reference to the underlying productive enterprise in which they represent ownership. If you saw the movie *When Harry Met Sally*, you'll understand the problem I am talking about. Sometimes you want what the person at the next table is having without any idea what it is. "Google at $700 a share? I'll have some of that!!"

Trust: In its formal sense, a trust is a legal mechanism whereby assets are set aside for a specific purpose, and managed and disbursed according to the provisions specified by the creator or grantor of the trust. Informally, trust is a critical component of your relationship with your financial advisor: something you give only after careful research and investigation, and which the advisor should continue to build and maintain over time. In either sense, trust involves a delegation of your intentions and wishes with respect to your money.

Withdrawal rate: This term describes the simple act of taking our own money from our savings or retirement accounts. There is much debate about the optimal withdrawal rate; i.e., the highest rate that will ensure our money lasts as long as we do. As is so often the case, simplicity trumps sophistication; keeping your annual withdrawal rate at approximately 4 percent of your initial balance in the account is a good all-weather strategy.

Works Cited

Allianz Life Insurance. *Report on Women, Money & Power*. Minneapolis, MN: Allianz, 2006.

Babcock, Linda, and Sara Laschever. *Women Don't Ask: Negotiation and the Gender Divide*. Princeton, NJ: Princeton University Press, 2003.

Barber, Brad M., and Terrance Odean. "Boys Will Be Boys: Gender, Overconfidence, and Common Stock Investment." *Quarterly Journal of Economics*, (April 20, 2000), http://papers.ssrn.com/sol3/papers.cfm?abstract_id=219240 (Revised September 3, 2008).

Black, Hilary, ed. *The Secret Currency of Love: The Unabashed Truth about Women, Money, and Relationships*. New York: William Morrow, 2009.

Blayney, Eleanor. *Home Budget Workbook: A Straightforward Guide to Create and Maintain a Practical Budget*. White Plains, NY: Peter Pauper Press, 2010.

Bogle, John C. *Bogle on Mutual Funds: New Perspectives for the Intelligent Investor*. Burr Ridge, IL: Irwin Professional, 1994.

Brafman, Ori, and Rom Brafman. *Sway: The Irresistible Pull of Irrational Behavior*. New York: Doubleday, 2008.

Calligaro, Julie A. *Arranging Your Financial and Legal Affairs: A Step-By-Step Guide to Getting Your Affairs in Order*. Taylor, MI: Women's Source Books, 1998.

Commission on Thrift. *For a New Thrift: Confronting the Debt Culture*. New York: Institute for American Values, 2008.

Corbett, David. *Portfolio Life: The New Path to Work, Purpose, and Passion After 50*. San Francisco: Jossey-Bass, 2007.

Crittenden, Ann. *The Price of Motherhood: Why the Most Important Job in the World Is Still the Least Valued*. New York: Henry Holt and Company, 2001.

DiCosmo, LouAnn. "Warren Buffett Invests Like a Girl." *The Motley Fool*, (March 20, 2008), http://www.fool.com/investing/value/2008/03/20/warren-buffett-invests-like-a-girl.aspx (accessed December 3, 2009).

Duerk, Judith. *A Circle of Stones: Woman's Journey to Herself*. San Diego, CA: LuraMedia, 1989.

Ellis, Charles D. *Winning the Loser's Game: Timeless Strategies for Successful Investing*. New York: McGraw–Hill, 2009.

Farrell, Charles J. "Personal Financial Ratios: An Elegant Road Map to Financial Health and Retirement." *Journal of Financial Planning*, January, 2006.

Hartford Financial Services Group/MIT AgeLab. "Why Women Worry(SM): New Research from the Hartford and the MIT AgeLab Identifies Inflation, Health and Longevity as Major Retirement Worries for Women," July 22, 2008. http://ir.thehartford.com/releaseDetail.cfm?releaseid=323756 (accessed November 15, 2009).

Hurley, Joseph. *The Best Way to Save for College: A Complete Guide to 529 Plans*. 8th ed. 2008, http://www.savingforcollege.com/ (accessed November 12, 2009).

Malkiel, Burton G. *A Random Walk Down Wall Street*. New York: W.W. Norton & Co., 2003.

Mellan, Olivia, and Sherry Christie. *Money Shy to Money Sure: A Woman's Road Map to Financial Well-Being*. New York: Walker & Company, 2001.

______. *Overcoming Overspending: A Winning Plan for Spenders and Their Partners*. New York: Walker & Company, 1995.

Merlino, Nell. *Stepping Out of Line: Lessons for Women Who Want It Their Way in Life, in Love, and at Work*. New York: Broadway Books, 2009.

National Program on Women & Aging. "500 Women Speak Out: Financial Plans and 'Financial Planners.'" *Women & Aging Letter*, Volume 3, Number 2. http://isap.brandies.edu/womenandaging/speakout.htm (accessed November 15, 2009).

Perle, Liz. *Money, A Memoir: Women, Emotions, and Cash*. New York: Henry Holt and Company, 2006.

Schwab-Pomeranz, Carrie, and Charles Schwab. *It Pays to Talk: How to Have the Essential Conversations with Your Family about Money and Investing*. New York: Crown Publishing Group, 2003.

Sethi, Ramit. *I Will Teach You to Be Rich*. New York: Workman, 2009.

Shipman, Claire, and Katty Kay. *Womenomics: Write Your Own Rules for Success*. New York: HarperCollins, 2009.

Silverstein, Michael J., and Kate Sayre. *Women Want More: How to Capture Your Share of the World's Largest, Fastest-Growing Market.* New York: HarperCollins, 2009.

Steiner, Sheyna. "Why Retirement Is Different for Women," www.bankrate.com, April 5, 2009.

Tannen, Deborah. "Communications Matters 1: He Said, She Said." http://www.learnoutloud.com/Catalog/Social-Sciences/Gender-Studies/ (accessed November 12, 2009).

Trafford, Abigail. *My Time: Making the Most of the Bonus Decades After 50*. New York: Perseus Publishing, 2003.

U.S. Bureau of Labor Statistics. *Occupational Outlook Handbook 2008–09*. Washington, DC: USBL, 2008.

Vasileff, Lili A. "Women and Financial Empowerment: Why Women Are Statistically Behind the Eight Ball." *The 2nd Annual Financial Resources Guide by Garden State Woman Magazine, 2005,* http://www.divorcematters.com/article6.html (accessed November 12, 2009).

Warren, Elizabeth, and Amelia Warren Tyagi. *All Your Worth: The Ultimate Lifetime Money Plan*. New York: Free Press, 2005.

Whitman, Wynne A. *Smart Women Protect Their Assets: Essential Information for Every Woman About Wills, Trusts, and More*. Upper Saddle River, NJ: FT Press, 2009.

Women and Company. "Survey Reveals 58 Percent of Women Do Not Review Their Financial Situation." *Business Wire*, March 30, 2006.

Acknowledgments

Whenever my attitude about my life or work needs a tune-up, I remind myself of the story of the little girl who comes running out of her house on her birthday, full of joy and expectation, only to see a big pile of horse manure on the sidewalk. "That's okay," she says. "I just know there is a pony here somewhere!"

In writing this book, there have been times when it was hard to believe in or see the pony for the big pile of discarded ideas, chapters, and drafts that kept growing at my feet. Fortunately, in my career and in this enterprise, I have been supported by many people whose vision, optimism, intelligence, and faith remained strong when mine sometimes flagged.

To my women clients, Bev, Marge, Maryann, Pilar, Cheryl, Susan, Alison, Betty, Chris, Linda, Christina, Lisa, Betsy, Jody, Amy, Candace, Emily, Kate, Dede, Carole, Lea, Marjorie, Priscilla, Ellen, Gail, Carrie, Carol, Ann, Libba, Leslie, Carolyn, Deborah, Anita, Charlene, Sara, Mary Anne, Becky, Nathalie, Vivian, Shannon, Mary, Janet, Joyce, Rhoda, Paula, Diane, Margaret, Myriam, and Debra: thank you for sharing with me your unique perspectives on money, values, work, parenting, and life. Your questions and trust made me work harder and stand taller as a financial advisor, and made me believe, too, that there is something powerful in women talking to women about finance.

To my partners at Sullivan, Bruyette, Speros & Blayney: as the "three men and a lady," we worked hard to build something special and enduring. Thank you for your willingness to bring me to the table as a partner, even when I had no revenues—just lots of ideas and opinions—to offer.

To the publishing team at Highspot, who truly delivered on their mission of "bringing ideas to market": before beginning this project you took my Kolbe profile and thereby had me pegged as a "shiny object" person—someone who keeps picking up every shiny idea that catches her eye and thereby risks dropping them all. Thank you for helping me keep my book basket full, but manageable.

To Kevin Keller, CEO of the Certified Financial Planner Board of Standards, and to the Board's leaders and staff for their commitment to making the CFP® designation the standard of excellence in financial planning: thank you for letting me speak on behalf of the CFP® Board about a profession and a practice I am truly passionate about.

To the women in the financial advisory profession who have mentored, supported, and inspired me: Deena Katz, Alexandra Armstrong, Judy Shine, Karen Schaeffer, Elaine Bedel, Jocelyn Kaplan, Peggy Ruhlin, Marilyn Capelli-Dimitroff, Lisa Kirchenbauer, Patti Houlihan, Heather Locus, Marjorie Fox, Alexandra Armstrong, Margaret Welch, Jane Newton, Jan Conner, Margie Carpenter, Karen Tovey, Jeanie Schwarz, Mary Maginniss, Barbara Schelhorn, Pam Shortal, Kris Andrejev, Collette Kolanko, Jenn Quigley, Celie Powers, Diana Chambers, Peg Downey, Elizabeth Jetton, Chris Fahlund, and Dr. Katy Votava. I was once asked to make a list of the best financial planners in the country, and when I realized, after finishing my list, that 90 percent of them were women, I knew I had made an important discovery. Women have a unique and powerful wisdom that makes them great advisors on a subject that is every bit as emotional as it is technical.

To the great men of my profession as well: Mark Johannessen, Jeff Porter, Gary Ingram, John Bender, Stefan Prvanov, Ross Levin, Harold Evensky, Lou Stanasolovich, David Bugen, Chris Cordaro, John Ueleke, Mark Balasa, Jim Budros, Chris Dardaman, Ram Kolluri, Charlie Haines, Don Phillips, Mark Tibergien, Mark Hurley, Bob Winfield, Tim Kochis, Armond Dinverno, Glenn Kautt, and John Cammack. Your respect, advice, friendship, and example have been the mainstays of my professional life.

To Page and Patti, my oldest, bestest friends, who have patiently and lovingly listened to every single idea I've ever had.

Finally, to SM, philosopher, psychologist, engineer, executive, navigator, president, and leader, whom I am so lucky to call my friend: thank you for teaching the teacher that money is indeed just grease.

About the Author

Eleanor Blayney, CFP®, has worked with clients for more than twenty years to help them articulate and plan for their personal financial goals. As the only woman partner in a four-partner firm, Eleanor drew upon her female intuition, communication strengths, and facility for sustaining relationships to help build a wealth management firm that has served hundreds of clients around the country.

Well-known as a conference speaker and spokesperson to the press, Eleanor has played a pioneering role in building and shaping the financial planning profession. She has taught for the College of Financial Planning and has helped develop practice standards and ethical requirements for CFP® professionals in the United States and worldwide. Currently she serves as the Consumer Advocate for the Certified Financial Planner Board of Standards, reaching out to consumers to help them understand how financial planning and CFP® professionals can improve their lives.

In 2008, Eleanor established Directions, LLC, a financial advisory service for women, because women ask for directions. You can read more about this service at the company's website, www.directionsforwomen.com, and can reach Eleanor at eleanor@directionsforwomen.com.

Index